WHAT THE CHINESE
DON'T EAT

Xinran was born in Beijing in 1958 and was a successful journalist and radio presenter in China. In 1997 she moved to London, where she began work on her seminal book about Chinese women's lives, *The Good Women of China*, which has become an international bestseller. Her most recent book is *Sky Burial*.

ALSO BY XINRAN

The Good Women of China
Sky Burial

XINRAN

What the Chinese Don't Eat

The Collected *Guardian* Columns

VINTAGE BOOKS
London

For Mary Wesley – my mother-in-law who loved reading the *Guardian*

Published by Vintage 2006

2 4 6 8 10 9 7 5 3

These columns were first published in the *Guardian* newspaper between
2nd June 2003 and 9th September 2005

This book is published in association with Guardian Books.
Guardian Books is an imprint of Guardian Newspapers Limited.
The Guardian is a registered trademark of Guardian Media Group plc.

theguardian

First published in Great Britain in 2006 by Vintage

Vintage
Random House, 20 Vauxhall Bridge Road,
London sw1 2sa

The Random House Group Limited Reg. No. 954009
www.randomhouse.co.uk/vintage

A CIP catalogue record for this book
is available from the British Library

ISBN 9780099501527 (from Jan 2007)
ISBN 009950152X

Papers used by Random House are natural,
recyclable products made from wood grown in
sustainable forests. The manufacturing processes
conform to the environmental regulations of the
country of origin

Typeset by Palimpsest Book Production Limited,
Polmont, Stirlingshire
Printed and bound in Great Britain by
Bookmarque Ltd, Croydon, Surrey

Contents

Introduction   ix

Chinese whispers   1

Where the son shines   7

In the west, a kiss is just a kiss   11

Is there any female on earth who could meet the five male requirements of a good woman?   15

In a four-star hotel in China, one woman's cup of tea is another woman's daily wages   19

'Do the foreigners who adopt our girls know how to feed and love them in their arms and hearts?'   23

In China, god is god   27

Now women in China know what they have been missing, the pain is too hard to bear   31

Traditions may be dying out but forcing children to wash their parents' feet won't help   35

The Chinese are still obsessed with saving face   39

Chinese honesty means telling the bald truth   43

If it flies, if it swims, or if it has four legs but is not a table or chair, the Chinese eat it   47

New Year's Eve in Shanghai   51

Shanghai has a new skyline but why does the woman who used to clean my ears have a new face? 55

Chinese new year has suddenly made me doubt how well I know my own culture 59

As the sea rose, the cocklers rang their families in China 63

I may be Chinese but my knowledge is still just a spoonful of tea in the ocean that is China 67

What use is freedom and democracy to the poor if you can't sell it by the kilogram? 71

The story of the Red Guards, the forgetful ferryman, and the cat that reunited a family 75

They move millions to a new town, replant entire mountains – the Chinese are amazing 79

Twenty years after I first heard of it, I found myself scouring a Chinese street for a HongDu-Dou 83

The ghosts of Qing-Zang 87

A late-night knock at the door – is it the return of the Cultural Revolution? 93

If it says 'made in China' on the label, most Chinese just don't want to know 97

Chinese girls adopted by westerners highlight a vast cultural divide that must be bridged 101

A couple of unforgettable chickens reinforced my faith in human kindness 105

A shocking tale in a New Zealand bookshop is a
  lesson that hate is an emotion best forgotten — 109

The young do not understand the madness and
  pain of the Cultural Revolution — 113

My friends in China ask me to look out for their visiting
  children – but I have to draw the line somewhere — 117

Eat them, catch them, or look at them in an aquarium.
  But what fish are really best for is explaining life — 121

I used to think there were no good Chinese men,
  until a brief encounter at Paddington station — 125

Adjusting to life in London means roast pork, girls
  in smelly clothes and automated phone operators — 129

How China has embraced all the bright lights and
  overindulgence of a very merry Craze Mass — 133

In 1976 an earthquake in China caused double
  the death toll of the tsunami — 137

Receiving a handwritten card in this age of computers
  is one of the great pleasures in life — 141

Victorious Egg Festival, Sexual Hooligans' Day? — 145

The west ruined our self-confidence years ago — 149

The gap between western and Chinese paintings
  is as vast as that between the two cultures — 153

How to bridge the gulf between Chinese and
  western painting — 157

When Chinese art meets western culture, an
  inner world is revealed   159

China is my homeland. But these days I am   163
  lost in translation

There are still students in China who believe   167
  babies come out of their mothers' tummy buttons

The chatroom gives Chinese women a chance to   171
  be open and express their true thoughts

Socks are a status symbol – does that mean   175
  barelegged westerners are all peasants?

There is no point worrying about feeling down   179

English schoolchildren have shown me that China   183
  has much to learn about the joy of education

Ears, lips, fingers, toes: Chinese men used to check   187
  them all in the search for the perfect wife

The English break the ice by talking about   191
  weather, but the Chinese choose food

Why do old men, who need sticks to walk, open   195
  doors for healthy middle-aged women?

Even now, many Chinese find it impossible to see   199
  Mao as anything but a smiling presence

My mother's heart attack has shattered our   203
  dreams of finally getting to know each other

Introduction

The first time I came across the *Guardian* was in the 1970s in a foreign media research textbook. A tiny note followed the introduction: 'The *Guardian* is a left-wing newspaper, considered one of the top ten anti-Communist papers.' The Chinese media did, nevertheless, use the occasional article from the *Guardian* to illustrate their disapproval of Margaret Thatcher's foreign policy, including the Falklands War.

The *Guardian* was also on a forbidden media list at the radio station I worked at from 1989 to 1997. The list told us which western newspapers would attack China and should never be believed. Therefore I never thought that I, a Chinese woman – though admittedly one brought up with a flak-jacket to defend the *Guardian* and its influence – would ever have the opportunity to write a fortnightly column in this newspaper for more than two years.

What have I really liked about being a columnist for the *Guardian*? It's a hard question to answer; in the same way as it's difficult to know why I love cheese when most Chinese people don't. The first thing that comes to my mind is the impression that I got from the restaurants where the *Guardian* staff took me for lunch. These restaurants were not very grand – which matched my level of writing; they were not snooty – a Chinese woman was always treated as a welcome guest; they were European, but comfortable with different cultures – they were keen for me to write about the differences with China; and they all offered unforgettable tastes and I've always loved my food. Every meal replenished my energy for digging into my Chinese thoughts.

The second thing is to do with the male readers of my column. Since the publication of my books, *The Good Women of China* and *Sky Burial,* in over thirty languages, I have met so many female readers and admirers but not many male ones. Men don't read books by women, I have been constantly told all over the world. Why? Because most men believe only women with nothing else to do – housewives and prostitutes, for instance – have time to write books. I was also told that men prefer reading papers. This last idea rings true, judging by the responses I've had from my column, many more of which have come from men than from women. The first person to suggest I publish my columns together as a book was a British man. Also, the only two people I know who collected all of them are an Australian businessman in Beijing and a German journalist in Hamburg. Obviously this has been a real chance for me to learn what men think about Chinese culture.

The third thing I have liked is to do with the responses of some of the 100,000 families around the world who have adopted Chinese daughters.

Dear Xinran,

My daughter is seven. I adopted her when she was three. All I know is that she was abandoned at 18 months in Chengdu. For every child who finds a home, there are so many left behind. I think of what life will be like for the girls who grow up in institutions. And I always think of my daughter's birth mother and wonder if she has a huge hole in her heart through having to live without this wonderful child. I can't even imagine the collective sorrow all these birth mothers must feel.

Did you ever interview any of these women who were forced to give up children because of the 'one child' law? Is there any possibility of writing their stories? I know all of our Chinese daughters will one day be searching for answers.

Some families also sent videos to me with their adopted daughters' questions:

'Why my Chinese mum didn't want me?'

'Does my Chinese mum miss me?'

'What is Chinese culture? Why people say it is take-way? Is it true?'

So, apart from digging out my answers for them in my writing and my interviews in China between 1989 and 1997 when I was a radio presenter in Henan and Jiangsu, I also set up the Mothers' Bridge of Love, a charity which tries to bridge the gap between China and rest of the world, between the culture of one's birthplace and one's home, between rich and poor. I quickly became a builder with a lot of hard labour to perform, carrying books to family events, raising money and even holding costumes during performances of Chinese dance.

Each column I wrote provoked more questions and stories from my readers, driving me on to the next. One of my earliest columns started with how I got the first western kiss on my face from my students at London University. My writing is based on my own experiences and views, which have been 'weathered' by Chinese traditional culture and modern China. I have written about what the Chinese don't eat; why we see washing feet every day as so important; how the Chinese fish philosophy really helped my life choices; how my Chinese knowledge and language is lost in a fast-changing motherland; my conversations with a wild-flower seller at Xian about the punishments of opening the Terracotta Warriors; the football craziness at my radio station and home; and what makes a good woman in men's eyes. I have also written about many of my interviews with Chinese women; about how some tried to commit suicide; how some of them are struggling with modern life – including how to see sex; and how some still treat Mao as a Chinese God.

It was Clare Margetson, the *Guardian*'s women's editor, who started me on the path to this book. In the spring of 2003, she came to my office to talk to me about my first book, *The Good Women of China*. After just a few words from her, I opened my heart. She very successfully guided me to what she believed western readers wanted to know about China, without making me dizzy. (I still often get lost amongst the kind suggestions and guidance of westerners!) Clare and I went to China together in April 2005 with a group of western publishers and in Nanjing she asked me the question 'What do the Chinese NOT eat?'

What the Chinese don't eat . . . I had never thought about this. But I knew that there was saying about it: everything that flies in the sky which you can see, except airplanes; everything that swims in the river and the sea, except submarines; any four-legged things on the ground, except tables and chairs – that is what the Chinese eat.

Since I moved to London in 1997, and have travelled around over thirty countries, I have been asked so many questions like Clare's, such as :

'Are there any swimming pools in China?'

'Why do Chinese women wear stockings in summer?'

'Do Chinese people do Christmas shopping?'

'Why are the Chinese so different when they are in the media?'

'Why do the Chinese never say their own opinions in public?'

'Why do Chinese mothers always say their beautiful daughters are ugly in China?'

'What do Chinese university students think about where babies come from?'

This is a book about the answers in my *Guardian* columns to some of those questions, answers from a Chinese woman and the mother of a Chinese son.

Thanks to you from my Chinese heart – *XieXie!*

Xinran, 2006

2nd June 2003

Chinese whispers: When radio presenter Xinran got a letter asking her to help free a kidnapped 12-year-old child bride, she realised how little was known about the lives of real women in her country. So she resolved to tell their stories in her book, The Good Women of China

Early one spring morning in 1989, I rode my Flying Pigeon bicycle through the streets of Nanjing dreaming about my son PanPan. The green shoots on the trees, the clouds of frosty breath enveloping the other cyclists, the women's silk scarves billowing in the spring wind, everything merged with thoughts of my son. I was bringing him up on my own, without the help of a man, and it was not easy caring for him as a working mother. Whatever journey I went on, though, long or short, even the quick ride to work, he accompanied me in spirit and gave me courage.

'Hey, big-shot presenter, watch where you're going,' shouted a colleague as I wobbled into the compound of the radio and TV station where I worked.

My office was on the 16th floor of the forbidding, 21-storey modern building. I preferred to climb the stairs rather than risk the unreliable lift, which broke down frequently. When I arrived at my desk, amidst the large pile of letters, one immediately caught my attention: the envelope had been made from the cover of a book and there was a chicken feather glued to it. According to Chinese tradition, a chicken feather is an urgent distress signal.

The letter was from a young boy, and had been sent from a village about 150 miles from Nanjing.

I

Most respected Xinran,

I listen to every one of your programmes. In fact, everyone in our village likes listening to them. But I am not writing to tell you how good your programme is; I am writing to tell you a secret. It's not really a secret, because everyone in the village knows. There is an old, crippled man of 60 here who recently bought a young wife. The girl looks very young – I think she must have been kidnapped. This happens a lot around here, but many of the girls escape later. The old man is afraid his wife will run off, so he has tied a thick iron chain around her. Her waist has been rubbed raw by the heavy chain – the blood has seeped through her clothes. I think it will kill her. Please save her.

Whatever you do, don't mention this on the radio. If the villagers find out, they'll drive my family away.

May your programme get better and better.

Your loyal listener,

Zhang Xiaoshuan

This was the most distressing letter I had received since I had started presenting my evening radio programme, *Words on the Night Breeze*, four months earlier. During the programme I discussed various aspects of daily life and used my own experiences to win the listeners' trust and suggest ways of approaching life's difficulties. The programme was a new thing for everyone, myself included. I had only just become a presenter and I was trying to do something that hadn't been done on the radio before.

Since 1949, the media had been the mouthpiece of the Party. State radio, state newspapers and, later, state television provided the only information Chinese people had access to, and they spoke with one identical voice. Communication with anyone abroad seemed as remote as a fairy tale. When Deng Xiaoping started the slow process of 'opening up' China in the 1980s, it was possible for journalists, if they were courageous, to try and make subtle changes to how they presented the news. It was also possible, although perhaps even more dangerous, to discuss personal issues in the media. In *Words on the Night Breeze* I was trying to open a little window, a tiny hole, so that people could allow their spirits to cry out and breathe after the gunpowder-laden atmosphere of the previous 40 years.

The letter I received from the young boy Zhang Xiaoshuan was the first that had appealed for my practical help and it threw me into confusion. I reported it to my section head and asked what I should do. He suggested indifferently that I contact the local Public Security Bureau. I put a call through and poured out Zhang Xiaoshuan's story.

The police officer on the other end of the line told me to calm down. 'This sort of thing happens a lot. If everyone reacted like you, we'd be worked to death. Anyway, it's a hopeless case. We have piles of reports here, and our human and financial resources are limited. I would be very wary of getting mixed up in it if I were you. Villagers like that aren't afraid of anyone or anything; even if we turned up there, they'd torch our cars and beat up our officers. They will go to incredible lengths to make sure that their family lines are perpetuated so as not to sin against their ancestors by failing to produce an heir.'

'So,' I said, 'Are you telling me you are not going to take responsibility for this girl?'

'I didn't say I wouldn't, but . . .'

'But what?'

'But there's no need to hurry, we can take it step by step.'

'You can't leave someone to die step by step!'

The policeman chuckled. 'All right, Xinran, come over. I'll help you.' He sounded as if he was doing me a favour rather than performing his duty.

I went straight to his office. 'In the countryside,' he said, 'the heavens are high and the emperor is far away.' In his opinion the law had no power there. The peasants feared only the local authorities who controlled their supplies of pesticide, fertiliser, seeds and farming tools.

The policeman was right. In the end, it was the head of the village agricultural supplies depot who managed to save the girl. He threatened to cut off the villagers' supply of fertiliser if they did not release her. Three policemen took me to the village in a police car. When we arrived, the village head had to clear the way for us through the villagers, who were shaking their fists and cursing us. The girl was only 12 years old. We took her away from the old man, who wept and swore bitterly. I dared not ask after the schoolboy who had written to me. I wanted to thank him, but the police officer told me that if the villagers found out what he had done, they might murder him and his family.

The girl was sent back to her family in Xining – a 22-hour train journey from Nanjing – accompanied by a police officer and someone from the radio station. It turned out that her parents had run up a debt of nearly 10,000 yuan searching for her.

I received no praise for the rescue of this girl, only criticism for 'moving the troops about and stirring up the people', and wasting the radio station's time and money. I was shaken by these complaints. A young girl had been in danger and yet going to her rescue was seen as 'exhausting the people and draining the treasury'. Just what was a woman's life worth in China?

This question began to haunt me. Most of the people who wrote to me at the radio station were women. Their letters were often anonymous, or written under an assumed name. Much of what they said came as a profound shock to me. I had believed that I understood Chinese women. Reading their letters, I realised how wrong my assumption had been.

My fellow women were living lives and struggling with problems I had not dreamed of.

Many of the questions they asked me related to their sexuality. One woman wanted to know why her heart beat faster when she accidentally bumped into a man on the bus. Another asked why she broke out into a sweat when a man touched her hand. For so long, all discussion of sexual matters had been forbidden and any physical contact between a man and woman who were not married had led to public condemnation – being 'struggled against' – or even imprisonment. Even between a husband and wife 'pillow talk' could be taken as evidence of delinquent behaviour and, in family quarrels, people would often threaten to denounce their partners to the police for having indulged in it. As a result, two generations of Chinese had grown up with their natural instincts in confusion.

I myself was once so ignorant that even at the age of 22, I refused to hold hands with a male teacher at a bonfire party for fear of getting pregnant. My understanding of conception was gleaned from a line in a book: 'They held hands under the light of the moon . . . In spring they had a bouncing baby son.' I found myself wanting to know much more about the intimate lives of Chinese women and decided to start researching their different cultural backgrounds.

Old Chen was the first person I told about my project. He had been a journalist for a very long time and was highly respected. I often consulted him about my work, out of deference to his seniority, but also to draw on his considerable experience. This time, however, his reaction surprised me. He shook his head and said, 'Naive!'

I was taken aback. Was I wrong? Why was it so naive to want to understand Chinese women?

I told a friend who worked at the university about Old Chen's warning.

'Xinran,' he said, 'have you ever been inside a sponge cake factory?'

'No,' I replied, confused.

'Well, I have. So I never eat sponge cake.' He suggested that I try visiting a bakery to see what he meant.

The manager at the bakery did not know why I had come but he was impressed by my devotion to my job: he said that he had never seen a journalist up so early to gather material. It was not yet fully light; under the dim light of the factory lamps, seven or eight female workers were breaking eggs into a large vat. They were yawning and clearing their throats with a dreadful hawking noise. The intermittent sound of spitting made me feel uneasy.

As I left the factory, I remembered something a fellow journalist had once told me: the dirtiest things in the world are not toilets or sewers, but food factories and restaurant kitchens. I resolved never to eat sponge cake again, but could not work out how what I had seen related to the question of understanding women.

I rang my friend, who seemed disappointed with my lack of perception.

'You have seen what those beautiful, soft cakes went through to become what they are. If you had only looked at them in the shop, you would never have known. However, although you might succeed in describing how badly managed the factory is and how it contravenes health regulations, do you think it will stop people wanting to eat sponge cake? It's the same with Chinese women. Even if you manage to get access to their homes and their memories, will you be able to judge or change the laws by which they live their lives? Besides, how many women will actually be willing to give up their self-respect and talk to you? I'm afraid I think that your colleague is indeed wise.'

This is an edited extract from *The Good Women of China*.

11th July 2003

Where the son shines. She is an icon in China, a pioneering journalist and its first radio agony aunt. In 1997 she moved to London to write the haunting stories she had heard into a book. In the first of a fortnightly column, Xinran finds out why for so many a boy is worth more than a girl

A few months ago I had a coffee and a chat with a friend, who mentioned that a friend of hers was unhappy because his wife was pregnant with a girl. This meant that his family's first seed had not been properly sown. When I heard this I could not quite believe my ears: 'Is he British? A modern, educated westerner?' 'Absolutely,' she replied. This surprise set me thinking: so idolising men and degrading women was not a Chinese characteristic, or a problem in developing countries. Time, civilisation and modernisation had brought progress to the world, but they had not brought everyone's education and consciousness into the 21st century.

At a launch party for my book, a reporter from a women's magazine gave me a newspaper article on the imbalance of the sexes among young people in China; she hoped that I would write a personal view on the subject. I do not usually read the papers while surrounded by bouquets of flowers and fine wines: first, wine is apt to make the words on the newspaper 'come in pairs', second, the notes of congratulation in bouquets are liable to turn a person of no account into a universal expert. But all my resolutions went out of the window with the headline: Chinese men cannot find wives. Was this true? Were we Chinese really facing a breaking off of the family line?

By the time I got home, while lights were still burning in thousands of London homes, all my Chinese friends were asleep, dreaming the dreams of a Nanjing summer. I could only just restrain my flustered heart and impatient fingers.

At two in the morning, I got through to a friend who works in an important government office. Her telephone manner was businesslike. 'Xinran, you're still so incorrigibly naive, so easily swayed by propaganda in the western media.

'It's true that for many male graduates, especially in the more developed regions, lack of power or money mean it's hard to find a wife. There are too few girls in the cities and the quality of country girls is too low. There's no way round it, we have controlled our population explosion but we have no way to stop people from trying to control the sex of their child, in order to "keep the family incense lit". In the big cities the ratio of 20 boys to every girl is far, far bigger than the 6:1 we had originally reckoned on.

'Of course the government has a firm policy against this; we had one before and we have one now. But how many people will really take notice? Who can resist traditional values, and parents who believe property is "an encouragement and reward for sons and grandsons". You know Xinran, journalists discovering problems and governments solving them are two very different things.

'We sent many officials to explain to people at the grassroots level that there is no distinction between the sexes in our economic and taxation policies, and that if we get an imbalance in the population, everybody's "incense will go out"; some peasant cadres even tore down the houses of families who had had six girls and still wanted to have a son. But if you look at the banquets that are given at the birth of a son, and the personal damage and divorce cases that result from giving birth to a girl, it will be clear to you that in human behaviour, "It is easier to clean up the leaves than the roots."

'What is to be done? Relax the policy of population control? Xinran, has western so-called civilisation turned you into an idiot? You know we have always allowed an extra birth in the countryside, sometimes even three. There can only be the most rigorous implementation of the one-child policy in the big cities, and this is why our city boys can't find wives. But can the few developed cities with their limited economic development support so many impoverished peasants? If China becomes like Somalia or the Sudan after we relax the population control policy, what will we do? Won't future generations curse our name? Better to have young men with problems finding a wife, than leaving future generations of women with nothing with which to feed or clothe their children.

'Don't fret for no reason, Xinran; we Chinese won't be left without a future, people learn best from their own hardships. Yes, yes, I agree with you, the price of this lesson is too high, and too painful.

'Is your boy PanPan well? Don't worry, you can have my daughter as a daughter-in-law, we have the "golden girl" that everyone's trying to get. And how's your book doing? Do the foreigners believe it? To be honest, Chinese women in the few generations before us have had it so hard that even their own children don't dare believe it.

'All right, go and get some sleep. I have to go to a meeting. Thank you.'

When I put down the phone, I suddenly felt a great distance between China and the rest of the world. China has been striding forward towards today at such a quick pace that she has had no time to appreciate the historical scenery, to think about her fellow-travellers through history, or even to consider whether we should give our battle-weary bodies a rest, after exhausting ourselves with the inner and outer conflicts of the past 100 years.

When I took up my pen and wrote down what I had learned, I found that there were none of my own views in it, but everything I want to say was already there. I thought about this English gentleman who wanted to have a son: maybe he believes in the traditional Chinese view that 'there are three sorts of unfilial behaviour, of which the worst is to have no heirs'. But without a doubt, he needed somebody's daughter to give him a son.

25th July 2003

In the west, a kiss is just a kiss. If only that were true where I come from

I am a Chinese woman. According to our culture, which is very closed and hidden, we don't kiss each other. The only exceptions are for little children and married couples in bed. Two years ago, while I was teaching Chinese culture at London University, I told my students: 'Don't kiss me, please. I am Chinese and not used to being kissed.' But my traditional Chinese reserve was overturned by my students in the space of an hour.

It was my birthday and I was giving a summer course. I was running late, which is unusual as I always liked to be the first person in the classroom so that I could say hello to my students one by one when they came to their lesson. When I rushed in, everybody was there already, all 22 of them, standing by the door instead of sitting. Suddenly they came to me and kissed me on my face one by one. 'Happy birthday, Xinran!' they said. I knew I shouldn't complain when they gave me a kiss as a birthday present, but we had to start our lesson at once because I had so much to teach them in their short course.

During the lesson I felt that something was up with my students, but I could not find out what it was while I devoted myself to teaching. Forty-five minutes later, at the end of the period, one student stood up and said, 'Xinran, would you like to go to the toilet?'

'What? Why? Oh, come on, this is my own business, I don't need you to make suggestions about the toilet, do I?'

More and more voices spoke out. 'Come on, Xinran, you should go and relax on your birthday!'

'What's wrong with you all?' I was totally lost.

They started laughing and had strange looks on their faces.

'OK, I am going! I can't believe all of you force your teacher to go to the toilet on her birthday!' I thought they wouldn't calm down unless I went.

As I passed through a long hall full of other students, more laughter followed my steps.

'Oh my God!' I saw myself in the mirror. My face was covered with colourful kiss marks. They had been there throughout the 45 minutes I was teaching my colourful-lipped students.

I went back to the classroom in tears. My students were waiting for me quietly. I stood there and faced them without a sound, and they looked at me with their watchful eyes. After a long time in silence I said, 'Come here, let me kiss you, now it's my turn.' I kissed them one by one with many thanks and love from my deep heart.

Since then, I have enjoyed this beautiful western body-language with people – but only in the west, not in China.

My neighbour, after hearing this story, asked me, 'But what's wrong with kissing?'

In the west no one can believe that kissing has cost the lives of many Chinese women. When I was working as a radio presenter in Shanghai, I once received a suicide note from a 19-year-old girl. She wrote:

Dear Xinran,
Why didn't you reply to my letter? Didn't you realise that I had to decide between life and death?

I love him, but I have never done anything bad. He has never touched my body, but a neighbour saw him kiss me on the fore-head, and told everyone I was a bad woman. My mother and father are so ashamed.

I love my parents very much. Ever since I was small, I have hoped that they would be proud of me, happy that they had a clever, beautiful daughter rather than feeling inferior to others because they did not have a son.

Now I have made them lose hope and lose face. But I don't understand what I have done wrong. Surely love is not immoral or an offence against public decency?

I wrote to you to ask what to do. I thought you would help me explain things to my parents. But even you turn away.

Nobody cares. There is no reason to go on living. Farewell, Xinran. I love you and hate you.

A loyal listener in life, Xiao Yu.

Three weeks later, after she died, Xiao Yu's first letter begging for help finally arrived.

8th August 2003

Is there any female on earth who could meet the five male requirements of a good woman?

When I was doing my radio phone-in programme, I used to get so many calls and letters complaining about how difficult it was to be a good woman. I wanted to know why, so I did some research. I asked my male listeners two questions: 1) How many good women have there been in your family? 2) What is your view of a good woman?

Three weeks later I had received nearly 1,000 replies. Fewer than 20 of them said that they had had good women in their lives. I was shocked. I could not understand why – until I read the five requirements for a good woman that they gave in their letters.

A good woman, they thought, should 1) never go out and express her views to society; 2) provide a son for her husband's family tree; 3) never lose her temper and always be soft and smile at her men; 4) never burn food when she cooks and never mix colours when she washes; 5) be good in bed and have a good figure to show off.

I could not and still cannot imagine how many women in this world could match up to that standard. I realised that I for one was certainly not a good woman in most Chinese men's eyes. Because I had a well-known talk show, I was 'too open to be good'.

At that point, I thought there must be something wrong with Chinese culture and education, which could not make men and women equal. Then last year I met a Chinese man who grew up in the west. I asked him what his view of a good woman was. His answer was exactly the same as that of the un-western-educated Chinese men.

I realised that no degree or PhD could change a traditional view. Did we realise, I asked, how high a price women who wanted to be good paid for this stand?

Someone sent me the diary of a dying Chinese girl back in 1990. Her father abused her. When she asked for help from her mother, she was told to 'be quiet', otherwise people would call her a bad woman. The only way for the poor girl to avoid her father's attacks and still 'be a good girl' was to harm herself so that she could be sent to hospital, where she would be safe. One day she found that the touch of a fly was so much more beautiful than that of a human that she tried to keep a fly as a pet. She was so frightened at the thought of being sent home that she killed herself by rubbing a dead fly into the cut in her arm. Her name was Hong-Xue; she was 17.

In 1995 I was asked for help. A married couple in the countryside could not have a baby. It had been nearly three years. I could hardly believe the reasons they gave me: they never touched each other during their marriage.

I asked the man: 'Have you ever wanted to touch your wife?' 'Yes, all the time.' 'Why haven't you?' 'I want to be a good man.' His voice was very low.

'Do you know the difference between a 'husband' and a 'man' with a woman?' He did not say anything.

I turned to his wife: 'Have you ever wanted to be hugged and kissed by him?' 'Why do you ask me this? I am a good woman, as everybody knows in our village.' From her eyes I could see I was a 'bad woman'.

I asked in a more diplomatic way. 'Do you know where you are from?' She looked at me as if I was stupid. 'From my parents.'

'Do you know why and how?'

'They sleep together.'

'Do you believe they lay there without touching each other?'

'How could I know? Why do you ask me about such sexual hooligan things?' I could see anger in her eyes now.

'OK, OK, do you know how pigs and chickens produce their babies?' I felt so sorry to ask her this, but I had to. 'Of course! But they are animal, and we are . . .' She did not finish her sentence.

'Yes, we are a kind of animal too.' I was sure she had got it by now. To be certain, I drew a picture to show them what should happen when a married couple sleep together. Neither of them looked at my drawing, but they picked it up and left. Eighteen months later, they came to visit me with their lovely baby boy.

I think if a woman knows how to love, how to feel love and how to try to love, she is a good woman.

By the way, I have put the same question to western men over the past year. They differ on just one point: a good woman does not need to provide a boy for the family tree – *but* she should be beautiful and clever. Even more requirements than from the Chinese men! Is it possible for anyone to be a good woman?

29th August 2003

In a four-star hotel in China, one woman's cup of tea is another woman's daily wages

I was in the second-floor coffee shop of the Grand Central Hotel in Nanjing last year, waiting for the director of my old radio station. I had all my attention concentrated on my reading, when a voice spoke in my ear: 'Are you Xinran?' A cleaner was standing before me. She was polishing the dazzlingly bright metal railing beside me with a cloth, but her eyes were fixed on me.

'Yes? I'm Xinran. Is there something I can do for you?'

'No, nothing, I just wanted to tell you that the cup of tea you're drinking costs as much as my whole family earns in a day.' She turned her back on me and left.

I was stupefied. That cup of tea cost 15 yuan (£1.15) and it was the cheapest beverage in the four-star hotel. I am not wealthy: in a place like this, I could only be a tea-drinker, but she said I was drinking the daily income of her entire family. The cleaning woman and her words lingered on in my mind.

Two days later, I stopped her politely as she was leaving by the back door of the hotel. 'I saw you were at work at six o'clock this morning,' I said. 'That's really hard work.'

'It's nothing. I'm used to it. There are people who'd love to find hard labour like this and can't get it!' She told me she'd been working eight hours a day at the hotel for the best part of a year. 'Is it tiring?' I asked.

'How could it be anything else? There are a lot of cleaners in this hotel – you might not think there was that much for any one person to do, but none of us dares to stop and rest, and after eight hours we're too tired to move. But my child, my husband and the two old folk all have to eat, so I have to go to the market to buy vegetables, cook supper and do the housework.'

She said none of the cleaners took the half-hour break they were entitled to because they were scared. 'We may just get 15 yuan for a day, but we're paid by the day, and I can't do weekends either. But it was hard enough to get this job. My husband's been laid off too. If neither of us does anything, what is the family supposed to eat, and how will we get the child to school?'

They would need a huge sum of money to send her six-year-old to school the following year, she said. 'Isn't there a system of compulsory education now?' I asked.

'It says in the papers that there's compulsory education, but what school doesn't demand support fees? That's 4–5,000 yuan at the least – 10,000 for some – and no school if you don't pay. But how can a child manage without school?'

I asked her if she liked her work. 'What does it matter? I've done well to have found this job, so many can't even do that. You go to the labour exchange and look at all those people searching for a job. If an employer comes in, the people looking for work are desperate enough to tear him to pieces. There are too many out of work these days.

'I got someone to fix [this job] for me. The first three months of my wages weren't enough to cover the "connection fees". And I have an advantage – I'm young. The really sad ones are the women of 40 and 50 who lose their jobs: people looking for workers think they're too old. The insurance people say it's not economical to insure older people. It's awful for the women laid-off – all those people like broken bricks thrown away by the roadside. You can't make them into a wall, at most you can use them to fill in the ditches by the side of the road, but far more of them are rubbish to be carted off to the tip.'

She said her husband hadn't found another job. 'He'd rather die than do all those low jobs. You know men, always thinking about their face. Still, life is hard enough already, if you don't iron out your own frown lines, nobody else will do it for you.'

I told her I was sorry. 'Not to worry. We're different. You live for the pleasant things in life, I live because I've no choice. Goodbye.'

This one sentence really gave me food for thought. Walking in the streets of London, watching women enjoy their shopping trips, I often thought of those women in China living 'because they must'. My only comfort was that in China, many women know how to 'iron away' the 'frown lines' of life.

If we say that my cup of tea was a day's wages for a woman worker, then how many days' wages are spent by the big businessmen and high-ranking officials who sit every day at the restaurant eating expensive mountain delicacies and seafood, with a new menu every day? What explanation can there be for this in a system whose slogan is to 'level out the differences between the rich and the poor'?

Translated by Esther Tyldesley

19th September 2003

Do the foreigners who adopt our girls know how to feed and love them in their arms and hearts?

Recently I received an email. Had I ever interviewed any women who were forced to give up children because of the 'one child' law, which China started in 1981? Yes, many.

One particularly painful memory stands out. On a cold winter morning in 1990, I passed a public toilet in Zhangzhou. A noisy crowd had formed around a little bag of clothes lying in the windy entrance. People were pointing and shouting: 'Look, look, she is still alive!'

'Alive? Was this another abandoned baby girl?' I pushed through the crowd and picked up that little bundle: it was a baby girl, barely a few days' old. She was frozen blue, but her tiny nose was twitching. I begged for help: 'We should save her, she is alive!'

'Stupid woman, do you know what you are doing? How could you manage this poor thing?'

I couldn't wait for help. I took the baby to the nearest hospital. I paid for first aid for her, but no one in the hospital seemed to be in a hurry to save this dying baby. I took a tape recorder from my backpack and started reporting what I saw. It worked: a doctor stopped and took the baby to the emergency room.

As I waited outside, a nurse said: 'Please forgive our cold minds. There are too many abandoned baby girls for us to handle. We have helped more than 10, but afterwards, no one has wanted to take responsibility for their future.'

I broadcast this girl's story on my radio show that night. The phone lines were filled with both angry and sympathetic callers.

Ten days later, I got a letter from a childless couple; they wanted to adopt the baby girl. That same day on my answer machine, I heard a crying voice: 'Xinran, I am the mother of the baby girl. She was born just four days before you saved her. Thank you so much for taking my daughter to hospital. I watched in the crowd with my heart broken. I followed you and sat outside your radio station all day. Many, many times I almost shouted out to you: "That is my baby!"

'I know many people hate me; I hate myself even more. But you don't know how hard life is for a girl in the countryside as the first child of a poor family. When I saw their little bodies bullied by hard work and cruel men, I promised I wouldn't let my girl have such a hopeless life. Her father is a good man, but we can't go against our family and the village. We have to have a boy for the family tree.

'Oh, my money is running out, only two minutes left, it is so expensive.

'We can't read or write. But, if you can, please tell my girl in the future to remember that, no matter how her life turns out, my love will live in her blood and my voice in her heart. [I could hear her crying at this point.] Please beg her new family to love her as if she were their own. I will pray for them every day and . . .'

The message stopped. Three months later, I sent the baby girl to her new family – a schoolteacher and a lawyer – with her new name 'Better'. Better's mother never called again.

Afterwards, I started to search for other mothers who had abandoned their girls. This spring, I talked to some near the banks of the Yangtze river. Did they not want to find out where their babies were? 'I would rather suffer this dark hole inside me if it means she can have a better life. I don't want to disturb my girl's life,' said one. 'I am very pleased for a rich person to take my daughter; she has a right to live a good life,' said another.

One of them asked me: 'Do you believe those foreigners who adopt our girls know how to feed and love them in their arms and heart?'

Two days ago, I forwarded the email below to my assistant, Leo, in China, with a message: Could we do something for the mothers of our Chinese girl babies? Leo replied: Yes! Give the mothers our email address. Let's try to build an information bridge for our girls between the west and China.

Dear Xinran, My daughter is seven. I adopted her when she was three. All I know is that she was abandoned at 18 months in Chengdu. For every child who finds a home, there are so many left behind. I think of what life will be like for the girls who grow up in institutions. And I always think of my daughter's birth mother and wonder if she has a huge hole in her heart through having to live without this wonderful child. I can't even imagine the collective sorrow all these birth mothers must feel.

Did you ever interview any of these women who were forced to give up children because of the 'one child' law? Is there any possibility of writing their stories? I know all of our Chinese daughters will one day be searching for answers.

Sincerely, Kim Giuliano, USA

3rd October 2003

In China, god is god. Or possibly an emperor. Or a communist leader. Or a rural husband

I got an email from an Irishman last week. He told me he has a Chinese girlfriend who is very beautiful with an extremely gentle and kind mind. But he cannot understand why she prays in front of Buddha at home every evening and goes to the Catholic church every Sunday. He has tried very hard to imagine how those two religions work together in her soul, but he can't work it out. He asked me if there was something wrong with his girlfriend.

My answer is: she is perfectly all right. She is not the only one who has two beliefs. There are even a good many Chinese women who believe in all the religions of the world. During my researches between 1989 and 1997 in China, I heard and saw so many Chinese women who were struggling 'to catch up' their beliefs after religious freedom was declared in 1983. Most Chinese people who prayed were only doing so to ask for wealth or other benefits.

I came across one Christian woman, who had one Buddhist grandparent and one Taoist grandparent. The two were constantly arguing. Away from the joss sticks, the woman had set up a cross. The grandparents constantly scolded her for this, saying she was cursing them to an early death. The girl's mother believed in some form of qigong [a form of meditative exercise similar to tai chi] and the father believed in the god of wealth. They, too, were always quarrelling: the woman said that the man's desire for money had damaged her spiritual standing, and the man accused the woman's evil influences of attacking his wealth. The little money this family had was spent on religious rituals or holy pictures, but they had grown neither richer nor happier.

Another woman I came across was said to be very religious. In public speeches, she would hail the Communist party as China's only hope; once off the podium, she would preach Buddhism, telling people that they would be rewarded in their next life according to their deeds in this one. When the wind changed, she would spread word of some form of miraculous qigong. Someone in her work unit said that she would wear a Communist party badge on her coat, fasten a picture of Buddha to her vest and pin a portrait of Great Master Zhang of the Zangmigong sect to her bra. Seeing my look of incredulity, I was told this woman was often mentioned in the newspapers. She was named as a model worker every year, and had been selected as an outstanding party member many times.

Are those Chinese women crazy? No, what they are is frightened since they lost their own human god. Over the last 5,000 years, the Chinese regarded their emperors and political leaders as their god, whose every word could mean the difference between life and death. In the early 20th century, China was plunged into chaos as the feudal system came to an end, and in all this bloodshed, the role of saviour was taken over by the warlords. They all understood that the Chinese could not do without their gods, as props to their spirits. No matter how different the theories of nationalism, democracy, socialism and communism represented by Sun Yat-sen, Chiang Kai-shek and Mao Zedong were, most ordinary Chinese in the period from 1920 to 1980 did not look on them as political leaders but as new emperors with modern names – and as their gods.

Given this, it is easy to understand the hysteria of the Red Guards during the Cultural Revolution, and the way intellectuals and peasants and workers alike unquestioningly obeyed their leader's commands, bowing their heads and allowing their gods to throw them into prison.

I know it is difficult for the rest of the world to understand this aspect of Chinese history. But having observed the zeal with which people from profoundly religious societies offered their most prized possessions – or even their children – to their gods in the past, you will understand the feelings of ordinary Chinese people who need a central power or belief for their security when they are not sure who should be their next god.

In my interviews with around 200 Chinese women, I found that for most uneducated rural women, their god is their husband. As for many young Chinese city women, they are waiting and seeing: as a Chinese girl in Nanjing told me, her belief will depend on what religion is in fashion next! So my reply to the Irishman was: please give your girlfriend more time to decide what she really believes.

17th October 2003

Now women in China know what they have been missing, the pain is too hard to bear

Why do so many women commit suicide in China? According to a report in the British medical journal the *Lancet* last year, suicide is China's fifth biggest killer, with women and girls most at risk. It reported that China is one of the few countries in the world where the female suicide rate is higher than it is for males. Twenty-five per cent more women commit suicide than men.

I don't know how many other countries this is true for; whether China is the only country in the world where more women commit suicide than men. And I don't know all the reasons why. But I do know through the many letters I receive some of the reasons why Chinese women give up their lives so easily.

First of all, in ancient times Roman gladiators killed and were killed for people's pleasure and their own glory, because people did not have the same respect for human life that they do today. Similarly, throughout Chinese history, there has been a culture of people killing themselves for the pleasure and honour of their family and for their own glory, for women to prove their honesty and, often, true love. This culture persists in many parts of China today, particularly in the rural areas of the south-west.

Secondly, quite a number of Chinese women would rather give up their lives than suffer from 'not being a good woman', according to the Chinese traditional role. For generations, having a good, clean name has been more important than human life itself. This is doubly true in the impoverished countryside, where, apart from housework, the importance of reputation is often the only thing they are taught.

What is a good, clean name? As I mentioned in a previous column, it means that a woman must be a virgin before marriage; that she should never be touched by a man apart from her husband; that she should never be seen alone with other men; and that she should not remarry or be with another man after her husband has died. In addition, many Chinese women in the countryside have a status much lower than that of men, even lower than big tools or property. When others do not treat you as a human being, it is difficult to know how to see yourself as one. Less than 100 years ago, the situation wasn't so different in the west.

But why do some Chinese women still feel hopeless, even though the country has been opened up and improved so much since the 1980s? I discovered the answer through a woman I met a few years ago.

I was sitting beside her in hospital. She was called Mei-Hua and had tried to commit suicide. I asked her why. 'Mei-Hua, I understood why you tried to kill yourself two years ago when you were in your village where you were bullied and abused by your ex-husband. You have a better life now in the city as a cleaner in a hotel – so why did you do it again?'

She looked at me: 'Why? I didn't know that there was such a different life here compared with my village. Then I thought about it all the time. Why have I not had the chance to learn to read and write in my life? Why do I have no right to choose whom I love – because I am a second-class citizen? Why did I have to give up my baby girl, while the daughters of city people dress beautifully and walk around arm in arm with young boys? How can I face them with the daily pain of my missing daughter?

'Why? What is wrong with my life? Why is my fate so poor? Why? Why?!'

Why? To be honest, I couldn't answer any of her whys. Mei-Hua and I both fell silent.

A child will not ask you for ice cream if she has never tasted it. People do not feel pain in their life when they have nothing to compare it with. Over the past 100 years, when the first lights of freedom and democracy came to China, many educated women suffered from what they knew but could not get in their lifetime. Over the past 20 years, when many peasants and farmers have flooded into cities to seize their first opportunity to make a better life, hundreds of women have found themselves lost in the same 'whys' as Mei-Hua's. I believe this is another of the reasons why Chinese women commit suicide.

Mei-Hua now has a job as a cleaner in a school thanks to her doctor. She can apparently now read basic children's books.

31st October 2003

Traditions may be dying out but forcing children to wash their parents' feet won't help

In China, state media have been reporting that school teachers in several places have been setting children the task of washing their parents' feet for their homework. It is an exercise designed to re-emphasise the traditional virtue of respect for one's elders, but it has met with some mixed reactions. The *China Daily* newspaper reported that at one school in Shanghai, most of the students did not complete the exercise and some of the parents were baffled by the task.

Washing feet is a part of the important 'water culture' in China. Traditionally, washing feet is done for three reasons: to clean dirty feet every day before going to bed (clean feet in bed is one of the most important things for Chinese at home); to improve health (the Chinese believe in massaging the feet during the washing, sometimes adding herbs to the hot water); and to help sex in marriage, which is why many rich people used to employ special foot-washers for their wives.

The Chinese believe that the foot is the lowest position in the human world. Therefore, we say, 'everything starts from your foot' – unlike the English 'from the bottom'. So washing the feet is a way of showing respect to previous generations or your husband. It also is a way of expressing personal regret if you are feeling guilty.

But why should washing feet form part of students' homework? I don't know why Chinese schools are picking up this piece of tradition to educate younger generations in a modern city such as Shanghai. But I do understand those Chinese parents and teachers who worry about what their children are losing – not only Chinese customs and traditions, but also how to think about life in a Chinese way, how to respect history and what previous generations have had to suffer in darker times.

A Chinese girl wrote an email to me a few months ago. She asked me: 'Xinran, I cannot believe that you said everyone – even my intelligent mother, who was a university professor – had to wave a little red book following the stupid emperor Mao during the Cultural Revolution. If she did, how could I respect her? Everyone knows the Cultural Revolution was a killing movement.'

I replied: 'Yes, everyone knows that today. But when you have been taught that Mao is our god and there is no other past, your eyes and ears are full of "red orders". You have no choice but to follow if you want to live – both for your family, and your baby children.

'Understand that it is easy to love and to give when you can do what you want. Your mother is a brave and intelligent woman because she knew how to give up her belief – for the family, for you. We have no idea how much pain she went through in that period. I am sure, because of her, you have this opportunity to study in the UK. You can think and ask me freely, something she could never do at your age.'

A friend in Shanghai called me last week complaining about her 22-year-old daughter. 'She has become a very western girl, changes boyfriend every week, goes to nightclubs and pubs. Does she eat with us at the weekends? Does she cook? No, she has no interest in our Chinese traditions of health and food any more. Every day she eats Kentucky, McDonald's, rubbish fast food. I don't know how to get her back, how to save her Chinese identity!' I didn't offer any suggestions because I still don't know how to make Chinese children seem Chinese in their mothers' eyes.

Do I think foot-washing could help the younger generation understand our tradition? Or should we push our children back to the old ways? Will today's young people forget their roots and become McDonald's boys and girls?

Not at all. Young Chinese will not understand the meaning of foot-washing when they grow up with factory-made nappies instead of hand-made clothes. No one will want to go back to the Stone Age when we have warm homes with modern heating.

The teens and 20s are a shaky time for everyone, wherever they are from. They won't understand what they need to take from traditions and ancestors, from other people and other countries and from their own experience, until they develop their own beliefs.

Young Chinese people now have opportunities given to them from all over the world, something previous generations never had. Once they have had time to explore these opportunities, I am sure they will develop new traditions of their own.

14th November 2003

The Chinese are still obsessed with saving face. Isn't it time we moved on and loosened up?

I have just got back from Iceland. It was a refreshing experience – not only because of the beautiful, cold weather, the open landscape, the northern lights and the way the coffee smelled on those dark mornings, but also because of the warm hearts of the Icelanders. They treat visitors as family – with their open minds and past full of pain and poverty. That is how I feel in China, except when it comes to talking about the past.

Almost every Icelander I met told me how poor their grandparents were: most had had to give away some of their children because they did not have enough to feed them all. Mothers had to count out the slices of bread for their daily rations. Girls married very early in order to give up their place in the home to their younger brothers or sisters. So many mothers had never known a life without worry.

There was no shame in their voices – they are proud of having moved on. They know how much they owe previous, impoverished generations. Their voices are full of respect and love for their poor parents.

Sixteen-year-old Fang, who is one of only two Chinese students in Iceland, told me that he was very surprised to find that Icelanders were so open and had no fear of losing face.

Iceland's past is similar to China's in many ways. But the Chinese have never opened up enough to tell people how poor they have been and how much they have suffered. Why? Because Chinese people cannot lose face. If you know any Chinese or have been to China, I am sure you must know how important saving face is for the Chinese.

In the (not too distant) past, and even today in the poorer areas of China, most people saved money on food in order to spend it on clothes – because at least no one would see your empty stomach. In rural areas people used to keep a piece of salty fat and smear it on their lips as make-up to impress others even if they had nothing to cook that day.

Once a man from the countryside had been educated or become established in the city, his peasant family would no longer be allowed to visit him, for fear of the man losing face in front of his new friends and acquaintances.

In the days when we were lost on some levels, many men had to kill themselves to keep their brave image, even as some parents forced their 'unclean' daughters – ones who had been raped or had lost their husbands or been touched by another man – to die to save the family's image.

When hundreds and thousands of Chinese starved in the 1960s, the newspapers continued to report large harvests, just so that we should not look unsuccessful. Even when we had a terrible earthquake in 1976, we hardly asked for any international aid in order to keep our self-respect.

Even though the numbers of Chinese women from rural areas committing suicide have topped world league tables in the past few years, many are still refusing to accept the truth to save their so-called liberated image.

So many city women also have to be traditional women at home. Even after a hard day's work, as hard as any man's, they end up doing the housework, looking after the child and the elderly relatives. Some people say this signifies 'equal rights' for their image as a good woman.

Think of those women who have had to give away their baby

girls. Few know who they are and no one holds them and soothes their broken hearts with warm, caring words because the families need a proud image for their family tree.

I don't know how many Chinese lives it has cost to save face in the past. I don't know how much time, energy and natural resources we are using up to maintain an image of power, just because we have not got enough international knowledge to educate younger generations to rid themselves of the vanity behind our image.

But I am glad to say that more and more young Chinese people notice the weakness of hiding behind such an image and have started questioning it: what is it for? I hope that soon we can be more free and open to tell people how much our Chinese grandmothers and mothers have given us through their suffering. The past is what makes up the roots of today; we need it for our future.

28th November 2003

Chinese honesty means telling the bald truth. But do we really want that degree of sincerity?

Last weekend, I went to the opening party of a Chinese student centre in London. We hoped to talk about what the greatest difficulties were for Chinese students overseas; how they could get in touch with western people; and what we should do to help Chinese girls' adoptive families in the west. But the first topic threw up so many problems that we ran out of time.

Some said they never understood what their professors and tutors meant by 'fantastic', 'wonderful' and 'excellent' – because even after being praised they found it hard to pass their exams. 'Why are they not honest with us?' they asked.

Some students doubted the western view of creation, and said they were always told to find points of argument against the eminent scholars and scientists who had proposed these ideas, and to come up with their own theories. 'How are we meant to argue against the great thinkers? Why do we need to be taught if we can come up with theories of creation by ourselves?'

Some students complained that western students could easily spend their entire student years talking, drinking, and making friends and lovers, while most Chinese students were fighting with their homework. 'How can we be the same age but live in such a different way?'

Some students felt sad about their classmates' families. Some westerners were so cold when they talked about their parents, they said, and some seemed polite and distant in the way they related to their families. 'Where else could we have a feeling of relaxation and safety as children, except at home with our parents? You can not be anything without family.'

We talked for more than three hours. In the end, they asked what I thought of their impressions. I told them three stories instead.

The first story I read from a funny book. One day, God sent a messenger to check on people's faith. The messenger returned and said Chinese people's faith was far greater than that of western people.

'Why?' said God. 'I haven't got enough time to look after the Chinese.'

'Chinese people always nod their heads when they read the Bible, but western people always shake their heads with doubt,' said the messenger.

'I need to give western people extra lessons on Sunday,' God said.

What was behind this story? Until the 1930s, the Chinese read from top to bottom, so people thought we nodded when we read, whereas westerners read from left to right and look as if they are shaking their heads in disagreement.

Our judgments are always coloured by our limited knowledge of the differences in the world.

I heard the second story from a teacher at London University. Four students – from America, Europe, Africa and China – are asked by a journalist: 'What's your personal opinion about the international food shortage?'

The American replies: 'What does international mean?' The European asks: 'What is shortage?' The African asks: 'What is food?' And the Chinese student says: 'What do you mean by personal opinion?'

Until the 1990s, the Chinese were closed in for thousands of years. We are not used to having our own 'personal' opinion.

But I am sure we know a lot that western people don't. This is why we are welcome to study here, and share our differences with them.

The third story is something that happened to me. In 1997, in my first week in London, I was stopped by a Chinese man in Leicester Square. 'Are you Xinran?' he said in Chinese.

'Aaah. . . um . . .' I mumbled.

'You are, I am sure!' he said, and was too excited to wait for my answer. 'Oh, it can't be true! You can't be Xinran!'

I didn't understand what he was talking about, but he kept shouting, in a street full of other Chinese speakers. 'Xinran, you can't be so old! Your face, why has it become so ugly? Oh, no!'

'I'm sorry, but I can't stop growing old,' I said, my face flushing.

He explained his pain at seeing me. When he arrived in Britain in 1989, he kept the last newspaper he had from China and stuck it on his wall to remind him of his home and language. He had not returned to China since. My face, 10 years younger, was in that paper, so he was shocked to see me in the flesh. What a typically honest Chinese man.

I asked those laughing students: 'Do you really enjoy this kind of "Chinese honesty"?'

12th December 2003

If it flies, if it swims, or if it has four legs but is not a table or chair, the Chinese eat it. Is that so odd?

I had a house-warming party this week. When it was all very busy I overheard a conversation about Chinese food:

A (a western woman): Could you tell me what Chinese people don't eat?

B (a Chinese man): Can I answer that the other way round?

A: Yes, of course. You mean what do the Chinese eat?

B: Listen carefully. Everything that flies in the sky which you can see, except airplanes; everything that swims in the river and the sea, except submarines; any four-legged things on the ground, except tables and chairs – that is what we eat.

A: What! Are you kidding?

B: No, I'm not joking.

A: Even cats and dogs?

B: Yes.

A: And foxes?

B: Yes. What's wrong with that?

A: But some animals are part of the human family – friends and pets. Their lives are not to be eaten.

B: What do you mean – animals' lives are not for eating? What did your western great, great-grandmother eat?

A: But we are living in a modern civilisation; we should respect natural life more than we used to.

B: Yes, you are right in some ways: if you are not hungry any more, if you have more living materials that can support your life.

This conversation triggered an old memory. In 1991, when

I interviewed some women in Mao Zedong's home town of Shaoshan in Hunan province, they asked me: 'We have heard how westerners eat cow every day, is it true? How? But cows feed humans with their milk and hard work. They are the hands of humans on the land, they are our lives, they even cry if you kill something in front of them, they have feelings.'

I knew that those people, whose agriculture depends on such animals, always send old or sick cows to the mountains to let them die there. I understand both ways of thinking – the Chinese peasants' and the westerners'. I told the women what I had read about disapproving western views on how Chinese eat cats and dogs. They listened to me with their heads shaking.

Then another snatch of conversation caught my attention at the party.

X (a Chinese woman): Oh, yes. I remember that restaurant is in Guangzhou, but I have never been.

Y (a western man): Why not? You are Chinese. I was told that it is the most famous dish in China. What's it called – 'Dragon Fights Tiger'?

X: Yes, or 'Dragon with Tiger'. It is very famous in south China, I know, but I really can't imagine I would enjoy it. I have never tasted either cat or snake.

Y: You are not typically Chinese, at least not a traditional one.

X: . . . not every Chinese likes to eat wild animals.

They were talking about a very famous restaurant in Guangzhou – the capital of Guangdong province. It has a speciality called 'Dragon and Tiger' which is made from a snake (dragon) and a cat (tiger) together in a kind of traditional canister dish. I was invited to try it in 1996, but I couldn't bear to either.

A western friend turned to me. 'Xinran, have you heard about the wild-food restaurant in Guilin [a beautiful area in the southwest part of China]?' I told her a story about some English friends. This middle-aged couple went to Guilin in late spring of 1998. One day, after a morning tour, their Chinese guide suggested they taste the local food. They went to a little wild-food restaurant by a beautiful river. A waiter talked them through their special menu: everything is alive, you can choose what you want from the animal yard by the kitchen, then they cook your choice in front of you.

The English woman was so shocked, she cried: 'No, no, please don't kill these lovely animals!'

The waiter was surprised. 'What? This is our business. What about our livelihood?'

'Yes, I understand,' the husband said. 'Let's see, is there any way we could consider both human and animal welfare?'

Eventually, they had a deal: the couple paid about $500 for all of the animals in that yard and let them free. The English couple then sat down to a vegetarian noodle lunch.

The next morning, the guide was woken by a telephone call. It was the owner of that little wild-food restaurant: 'Are you still with that English couple? Could you bring them back to my restaurant again? I will pay you double.'

'Why?'

'OK, just between us. I woke up this morning to find most of the animals that they freed yesterday have come back to the kitchen yard.'

9th January 2004

New Year's Eve in Shanghai: China's young are happy, care-free and changing fast

When the bells rang in the new year I was standing by a huge window on the 33rd floor of the Hong Kong SQ hotel in Shanghai with my husband and son. We pressed our warm faces to the cold glass to see the flashing and crowded street at the foot of the 50-storey building in the centre of this city of 20 million people. We stayed by the window for the last 15 minutes of 2003 and the first 20 minutes of 2004.

My son PanPan was really excited, and described the fireworks that lit up the city in many colours as a 'computer-designed picture'. I do not think the Chinese man who invented fireworks almost 2,000 years ago could have imagined that they would be a part of modern life in such a computer-controlled world. But I see more of China becoming part of today compared with the last time I went back, only six months ago. The two skyscrapers outside our window were not there last year. Roadside public welfare signs carrying the instructions 'Do not spit', 'Wash your hands before you eat' and 'Help needy strangers' are new. In the newly cleaned public toilets, which used to leave so many foreigners embarrassed, toilet paper has appeared.

We had our last meal of 2003 in a restaurant called Little South State (Xiao-Nan-Guo), which serves traditional Shanghai food, prepared according to ancient methods. My husband Toby, who has been to China at least twice a year since the early 90s, and is one of the few westerners who can eat most Chinese food, such as snake, ducks' feet and pigs' kidneys, was surprised by what he saw around us: there were many extended Chinese families (at least three generations together) having their New Year's Eve dinner in a place that used to be frequented by drunken governors and businessmen. People ate 'endless' dishes, which they ordered from a menu the size of a book. The 'drunk prawns' woke up and jumped out of diners' mouths, 'crab with eggs' was beautifully displayed, raw fish arranged like 'seasonal flowers' bloomed at the table and Shanghai veget-ables brought spring green to people's desires for the new year.

There were about 800 other diners with us, although that was far fewer than when we had dinner in Nanjing in the autumn of 2002. Then, 5,000 people sat down to eat together in a restaurant called Xiang-Yang Fishing House.

After dinner, we had to go for a walk to settle our full stom-achs. Along the Huai-Hai Road, adorned by neon lights and given voice by the crowds, we noticed that people in China are much more relaxed and happy today than we have ever seen them in the past. Toby said he would never have believed that the modern world would arrive in China so soon. He was very moved by Chinese people's behaviour at the new year: 'clean and not drunk' in the streets of Shanghai, because he knows the Chinese like to drink strong alcohol.

I hardly slept for the first night of 2004 because my mobile didn't stop bleeping with messages. Some were greetings from my friends. Some were from companies with information on shopping, travel and sales, offering body and foot massage, help with finding a lover, help with homework, house-cleaning, secondhand goods and weather forecasts. Some were from young people playing at 'new politicians': 'Don't say Bin Laden is too bad, don't think Bush is too kind, no oil no mad, let's see what those Americans mind . . .'; 'Think of Mao Ze-Dong, you won't be in pain (no more than the past); think of Deng Xiao-Ping, you won't lose money (get what you can get from opportunities coming your way); think of your parents, you won't be alone (in your family); think of love, you won't be a child (grow up for the future); think of me, you have someone to send this message to you at the new year . . .'

I learn a lot from my mobile when I am in China, about what young Chinese think, what they need and what they can do, from those short sentences on its tiny screen.

I flew back to London on January 2. There were so many Chinese in their late teens and early 20s in first class; they must come from rich or powerful families. How many of them can there be in China where 78% of the population are still peasants, half of whom have no education? I remember a student who came to Britain on a scholarship telling me his mother said to him on the phone from her small village: 'Take care, my son. Don't open the window when the plane is flying. It could be too windy.'

I really miss those Chinese mothers in today's China.

23rd January 2004

Shanghai has a new skyline but why does the woman who used to clean my ears have a new face?

I feel overcome by dizziness since my trip to China. I had felt dizzy a lot while I was there over the new year. I was made dizzy by the time difference, the busy schedule, parents' questions, brother's suggestions, friends calling; and the view of Shanghai, magically changed by the hundreds of new buildings erected in the last six months; the restaurant menus, now full of dishes I had never heard of; people's conversations in the street and on the radio, which sound so much more relaxed and free – pointing out some governor's corruption, judging a love affair, talking about sex, things I never dared talk about on the radio before 1997. I feel dizzy.

I almost fell over one morning when I took my son PanPan to Shanghai railway station for his short trip to Nanjing where my parents live. Every year I arrange some train trips to help PanPan's understanding of Chinese daily life. I don't believe PanPan will see China well enough if he always travels by plane.

Anyway, someone called my name as I dropped PanPan off and was heading out of the railway station. I looked around and couldn't find anyone I knew in the crowd. Then I heard a very loud voice in my right ear. 'Hi, Xinran, it's me, Li-Ping. Wait!'

There were groups of people all around: some peasants with huge amounts of luggage (they no longer seem to carry their belongings in dirty rolls) were eating some Chinese *baozi* (a steamed dumpling with meat inside); two country businessmen, in their suits, were talking about a factory deal through a cloud of smoke; a young western-looking woman with a red suitcase and green handbag was talking on her mobile phone; one city couple were helping an old man with his luggage. They must have just bought a lot of gifts for his trip. I couldn't see anyone among them that I knew. But it was without question my name.

'It is me, Xinran. I am glad that even *you* can't recognise me . . . ha . . . ha-ha . . .' The western woman was laughing at me. 'Are you sure you know me?' What a stupid question! I deeply regretted it.

'I am your friend, Li-Ping! We worked together more than four years in that old broadcasting house before we moved to the new building. Oh, I can't believe my face change has been so successful.'

The voice sounded familiar, but I really couldn't remember who she was. I have a friend called Li-Ping, who has a beautiful Chinese traditional face. But this woman had a typical western nose and golden brown hair. Something must be wrong. 'Oh, my dear, I haven't got time to play games with you. I have to catch my train. Let me give you some context . . . You must remember me, with my habit of "digging out people's ears".'

'Oh. *Oh* . . . *my God*, Li-Ping, it is *you!*' Of course I knew Li-Ping. She used to look forward so much to cleaning everybody's ears out in our radio station that sometimes she even paid people to let her do her ear-cleaning work. Yes, I did make some money from this. 'What's happened to your face? Are you OK? Where are you going?'

'Yes, yes. There is so much to say. Here is my card. Call me when I come back from my parents' home in Su-Zhou. It should be around new year. Good, good. I am so, so glad to see you again. I have to go now – my train leaves at 8am, and it is now 7.45. I must go. Let me give you a big kiss. Don't worry, I gave up my ear cleaning a long time ago, just a western kiss . . . Bye!'

Li-Ping ran to her platform.

Why had she done that? I have read about Chinese women paying high prices, both financially and physically, to change their faces.

I thought I understood them, because most just wanted a better chance of finding an attractive lover, or to improve lives that had been made more difficult by an ugly face, or to have a chance of getting a better job in those big companies run by male bosses.

But Li-Ping? She used to have such a beautiful face, one I was always jealous of. She was a famous radio presenter, who was great fun and loved running after men.

I looked at her card. She was working for a western trade company in Hong Kong. Is this why she had changed her face? For this western job? I don't know; I hope not. Such a strange feeling of loss: your good, old friend speaks and acts through a stranger's face.

I looked back at the railway station. I hoped that Li-Ping's parents would recognise their daughter. I felt completely dizzy.

6th February 2004

Chinese new year has suddenly made me know my own culture

'Happy Chinese new year!' '*Xin-nian-kuai-le!*' (*xin-nian*, meaning new year; *kuai-le*, meaning happy) has been said endlessly since January 14 – by people who think they understand Chinese culture, not by Chinese people themselves, that is. I thought it wasn't yet Chinese new year, but I was corrected at a Chinese new year party held at the beginning of January.

'Oh poor thing, you must be working too hard to remember that tonight is Chinese new year's eve.' People sympathised. I suddenly lost confidence in my knowledge of Chinese culture. I had to phone China. The only one who wouldn't laugh at me was my mother. 'Are you OK?' She sounded worried. 'Yes, I'm fine. I just want to confirm when Chinese new year is. Is it tomorrow?' (It falls on a different day each year, according to our traditional agricultural and lunar calendar).

'No, why? It was only two days ago that you wished us a good *xiao nian* ['small new year', a day for praying to the god of cooking]. Why do you wish to see seven days pass in 48 hours. Tell me honestly, are you well?' I felt really well after proving I was right all along.

A few days later, I went to Cornwall. Everybody greeted me with a 'happy Chinese new year'. I prepared a rich Chinese celebratory dinner for my British friends in a charming cottage near Penzance. With a glass of red wine and a half-drunken head, I called a friend to wish her a happy new year (China is eight hours ahead). We have been close since 1989 when I had my first radio programme.

you all right, Xinran? It's midnight here . . . I need to eep for tomorrow's big new year's eve show. Call me back in 10 hours if it is not urgent.' She sounded annoyed.

'Oh, no! I am wrong again.' I felt so hopeless. I couldn't tell my friends around the table that it was the wrong date; they were all drunk on Chinese happiness.

'I love Chinese new year and the way it goes on and on,' a British friend said when we had another new year's eve dinner, this time on the right day, January 21.

'When do the festivities end?'

'Traditionally, there are 15 days from new year until the Yuan-Xiao festival, when the first full moon arrives. The Chinese not only have a special meal called *yuan-xiao* for this; but most people also go out to Kan-Deng – in other words to see the lights, made out of hundreds of different materials such as clothes, bamboo, metals, and also electricity and computers.' I hated my poor English, which failed to describe how marvellous those lights can be.

'Lucky Chinese!' I could see how jealous my British friends were. 'Lucky Chinese?' For most Chinese, the 90% whose parents were farmers before the 1990s, this was the only time for them to have a rest during a whole year of physical hard work on the land.

'Is this the year the Chinese call "The Year of Monkey?"'

'Yes, it is.' I feel very sure about this answer.

'Which monkey is it?'

'What do you mean?' I had never heard such a question from my Chinese friends.

'Yes, you have "different monkeys", according to "Wu-Xing" – the five kinds of natural objects: metal, wood, water, fire, earth. You could have a wooden monkey, a fire monkey, etc. I read it in a newspaper.'

I picked up the phone again and tried to get help from two friends, one a radio presenter and the other a university professor. I obviously really need to improve my knowledge of Chinese culture.

'The monkey in the Chinese calendar is the same as the other 11 animals and matches the 12 sorts of times and years. The "wood monkey" possibly comes from the novel Monkey King. This is your question, isn't it? But you are Chinese.' The professor was talking in a funny voice, one I had not heard before. The presenter knew what I was talking about: 'I have read about that in foreign magazines. Just two days ago I read that it was Buddha who "set up" these 12 animals and matched them with metal, wood, water, fire and earth. You know that's wrong, Xinran. The 12 animals have been in Chinese recorded history for more than 3,000 years. Maybe this sort of street talk was in a western newspaper masquerading as Chinese culture?'

On the way back to London, my mobile rang. It was a message from a journalist: 'Happy Chinese new year, Xinran. How many monkeys are there in the Chinese lunar calendar in the whole of Chinese history.' I have no idea. I feel lost in my rich and deep culture again.

20th February 2004

As the sea rose, the cocklers rang their families in China. If only they had known about dialling 999

On February 5, 20 Chinese cockle pickers failed to return from work to celebrate the Yuan Xiao festival – the last day of Chinese new year. They never came back to their families and friends; to their motherland. They lost their life in the cold sea of a strange country.

They called their families and told them they were going to die when the freezing waves reached their chests. But they did not call 999 for help.

They were paid unbelievably little to do dangerous work for their bosses, who can make up to £20m a year. There are warning signs about 'quicksand and dangerous tides' near where they died, but they would not have understood them. They spoke no English. Yes, they may have been illegal, but they had basic human needs and should have had basic human rights to protect them. Why didn't they?

They were driven overseas by dreams of gold, and by ignorance. They came from a country that had no independent legal system before 1992, nor a welfare or social system. Their motherland is improving and developing now, but it is too late for them.

In 1997, when I came to Britain, I had the two most difficult months of my life. First was the house-hunting. It took me 45 minutes to get by tube from Bayswater to Queensway; in fact, you can walk from one to the other in five minutes. I found a very cheap place in north London. It had three bedrooms and one living room, and was occupied by 15 Chinese men who all worked in restaurants. They shared a tiny kitchen and a bath-room, but kept a storeroom aside to let to a translator who could help them deal with local government. I tried to explain that I was not well enough qualified to take their very cheap room, because my English was poor, I had no knowledge of the law and of how things worked in this country. I could not under-stand their papers from the Home Office. But I saw how scared, insecure and lost they were, the massive worry in their begging eyes and thirsty words. I felt so sorry I couldn't help them.

A few days later, I finally found a place near Queens Park, in north-west London. As I carried my luggage out of the tube station at 9.30 that evening, I was followed by four men and a big dog. After making sure they were indeed following me, I called 999 and asked for the police. 'Please help me; I am being followed by some men and a big dog.'

'Where are you? What do they look like?'

'I don't know where I am now, because I tried to get away from them, but I just left Queens Park tube station. On the right. But . . .'

'Just tell me – what can you see around you?'

'Sorry, I can't understand. You speak so quickly. Oh, my God, they are coming. Help!' My body started shaking; I could hear the men approaching me. I stood and tried to be still and thought very quickly how I could face this dangerous situation with my fighting skills, which I had learned at military university 20 years before.

I was lucky, the police arrived just as the four men stopped me. Afterwards, I thought about those Chinese men in north London, so I went to tell them about 999 and how useful the police had been. But no one was there. A man in the next door corner shop told me they had disappeared a few days before.

In the summer of 2002, I got a call from a stranger, a man

from Fujian province in south-east China. He was working in a Chinese restaurant washing dishes. He had fallen over in the street and injured his back; he could not see a doctor without an interpreter. His friend had found out my telephone number from a record of reservations at the restaurant. I went to see the man and sent him to hospital. On the way back he told me that, as a refugee, he had been given accommodation, shared with five other Chinese, and £48 a week to live on for the first few months or so. He was not allowed to leave Britain for 10 years. He was now working to repay his family's debt in China. I asked why he had not called the police when he was stuck, unable to move, on the pavement for three hours, while waiting for his friend to rescue him. He answered me with a very miserable look: 'Do you think there is a policeman or woman who can speak Chinese in London?'

On the seventh day after the death of the 20 Chinese cockle pickers, according to the custom of south-east China, I poured a glass of wine on to the earth to pray for them to go to heaven.

12th March 2004

I may be Chinese but my knowledge is still just a spoonful of tea in the ocean that is China

I find it more and more difficult to be a Chinese woman, both in the eyes of the west and of China. For westerners, I am not traditional enough; for people back home, my knowledge is not sufficiently up to date.

Years ago, I took English lessons in London. At one point my teacher asked who knew something about China. Three hands were raised.

A: Chinese respect food as their heaven, like strong tastes and slow cooking. They respect old people and serve meals to the oldest first.

B: Actually, most Chinese like sweet and light food cooked quickly. And people do not live with older generations any more.

'Which of you is Chinese?' my classmates asked.

A: I am Chinese.

B: Me, too.

Me: Me, three. (A silly phrase I had learned from my son PanPan.)

My teacher said: 'China is huge; there must be very varying lifestyles. Could all of you tell us some common things about China today? What about the single-child policy or the women's situation, for example?'

A: The situation for women has improved a lot since 1949. In my home town, everybody has the chance to get an education and a job.

B: Come on, that is not true. In our village, 75% of women

have not been to school; they work at home. And my mother, who is 48, can't read and write at all. But she is such a kind mother to our three boys.

A: Three children? Impossible! How old are you? How could your parents escape the one-child policy?

B: I am 19. The single-child policy doesn't work in our area. Some families even have six children.

A: Are you joking? They must be part of some minority nationality, such as Mongolian – then you can have as many as your family wants.

B: No, they are Han [who make up more than 90% of the Chinese population]. You can pay money to have extra children.

A: No, I don't think you can pay to get around government policy.

B: But I am here, my younger brother is in London too. Do you . . .

'OK, OK,' said the teacher, 'who is really Chinese, from mainland China?'

A: I am. I come from Chang-Chun, in the north-east of China.

B: Me, too. I come from Guang-Dong in the south-east of China.

Me: I come from Nan-Jing in the middle east of China.

The students asked why our knowledge of China was so varied.

China has 56 ethnic groups, each with its own history, language and culture. It is 42 times the size of Britain and its 5,000 years of history have nourished wealth equivalent to that of modern Europe and poverty as severe as that of the Sahara. About 1.3 billion people make things, trade, and love, too, in hundreds of accents, different languages, customs and cultures. Moreover, political control, policy, developments and living conditions are not comparable in different areas. This is why westerners hear such differing stories.

What I have experienced (as a journalist, radio presenter, columnist and guest professor) in China, whether in terms of environment or situation, can only be representative of a minuscule proportion, like a drop of water, or spoonful of green tea, in the big ocean that is China.

Also, I have been away for more than six years, while tremendous changes have been taking place daily. Every time I go back (more than twice a year), I learn new things, such as: how much more freely you can now talk about women's issues; how to talk to young women in a 'modern understandable language' with their ever-expanding vocabulary; how to choose dresses in new materials and styles; how to use the new radio and phone systems; even how to order dishes that are now served in new ways.

The more I learn, the less I really know the China of today. But, because it is so far away from the west, and few Chinese books and little Chinese news reach here, it is easier for westerners and ex-pats to become 'China experts' than it is for people back home.

I was interviewed once about Chinese women in New York. The interviewer was well known as 'a Chinese women's expert'. Before we went on air, I asked him how he knew Chinese women so well. His answer was relaxed, but it shocked me. 'I have been living in Chinatown for more than 15 years.'

'Have you been to China?'

'Not yet,' he said blandly.

'Do you have some Chinese women friends?'

'Er . . . oh, yes, I know some of their husbands. I have more than 20 Chinese friends; they work in Chinese restaurants . . .' If the red light had not flashed, I would have gone on with my foolish questions.

Afterwards an American woman told me that the interviewer had not talked in his usual way. She also said her husband had been disappointed: 'Xinran is too Chinese,' he had said.

7th April 2004

*What use is freedom and democracy to the poor if you can't
sell it by the kilogram?*

On the train to Gillingham last Saturday I listened to *Peasants'
Memory*, a CD from China sung by a group of women in a
gentle rhythm and with deep feeling. The sleeve notes said: 'In
the Chinese countryside, this song sold very well'.

I knew how much those peasants and farmers liked this old
1950s song about Mao Zedong's regard for his people, and how
they looked back at it with fondness, when I interviewed them
in the 1990s.

They were moved and warmed by the song because it showed
Mao's concern for them. But had he ever given them more than
just words? I did try to find out during my time as a radio
presenter in early 1990s with my women's talk show. I was a
little bit surprised by a woman in Shaaxi in 1989. She, with her
deaf-mute husband, and three daughters, all under their teens,
lived in a poor, empty, muddled house which had a hole in the
roof covered by a piece of plastic paper, but had Mao's picture
on the wall.

She told how much she missed Mao: 'He was such a kind
person who understood us poor peasants.'

My father told me it was only Mao who rescued us from a
war that lasted years, otherwise we could have lost more lives
in the fighting. I don't know very much about that period. But
I know that when I was little sometimes we had a poor harvest,
and then Mao would send food. But now who cares about the
poor low peasants?

I couldn't understand why such a large number of people

followed Chairman Mao, but in such a short time it had changed, and no one carried such kindness to our peasants at all. I couldn't give her my thoughts, maybe I couldn't have any, because my thoughts were limited by a different time and experience, and a different life.

In 1992, I was quite shocked by another woman in her 40s, called Xie Dong, meaning 'Thanks Mao', named by her mother in 1950s. She said her mother gave her this name because it was the first time for women in that area to have the right to name their children and keep their own name after marriage.

I asked her 'Do you believe Chairman Mao liberated women?'

'No question about that!' Her voice was so determined.

'But why do you still live in such poor conditions, still no electricity and running water more than 30 years after his rule?' I pointed to her unbelievably poor house.

'This is not his fault. This is because of those corrupt officers! He didn't know. He was so old and sick . . .' She sighed.

Partly, she was right. Since the 1990s, the Chinese had been encouraged to give alms to poor peasants at every traditional festival and national date, but most of their contributions were taken to those officers' relatives' pockets; very little reached the poor in the countryside.

This kind of conversation helped me understand a little bit more than before why Mao – who in many people's eyes, especially in the west, is seen as a bad man who made fools of his people, killed millions and let China fall into poverty is still loved and revered by many Chinese – not only peasants and farmers. Because he brought peace to China after the 40 years' war (1910–1949), understood and gave what those peasants and farmers (more than 90% of the population by then) needed.

In 1995, I asked a woman who lived near Mao's hometown – Shaoshan: 'If you had a choice of three things which one would you take: money and land, husband and children or democracy and freedom?'

She batted her eyes and said 'Money and land? That always belongs to men; husband and children are women's life, my god and duty. What was the last thing you said? Some oil and pigs? How much per kilo is it?' she asked.

(In Chinese, 'oil' – 'you', is pronounced the same as part of the word for 'freedom' – 'zi-you', and 'pig' sounds the same as part of the word for 'democracy' – 'min-zhu'.)

Can we really help someone who doesn't have adequate living conditions and education to understand concepts like 'political freedom and democracy'?

Anyhow, I'm delighted that in Wen Jia-Bao's report to the opening National People's Congress, the prime minister of China pointed out the gap between city and rural life. The government seems to be starting to pay more attention to the poor west of the country: peasants' and farmers' lives could be improved by cutting tax over the next five years and 1.2bn RMB would be spent on schooling in the area. If it works.

16th April 2004

The story of the Red Guards, the forgetful ferryman, and the cat that reunited a family

Mr Chopsticks had a cat called Mimi – a very Chinese lady cat. Mimi was very frightened when the Red Guards came to the house and destroyed everything of value – original paintings by famous artists such as Xu-Beihong; Tang and Song dynasty potteries; Ming dynasty furniture. But she helped Mr Chopsticks hide some old family photos in her basket.

A few days later, the Red Guards returned to 'clean up' the empty house in which only beds, tables, chairs and some simple cooking utensils remained. One guard noticed they hadn't checked Mimi's bed, so he stepped on her tail and Mimi cried and ran away. They found the photos hidden in her bed. They were so angry that they caught Mimi, and gave her a 'revolutionary lesson': they hung her from her front feet in the tree in Mr Chopsticks' yard, with a notice reading 'Capitalist Cat' tied to her collar, poured chilli sauce into her tiny nose and beat her body with a leather belt. A few minutes later Mimi couldn't miaow any more. Mr Chopsticks was forced to watch to the very end, when the soldiers took her away. His heart ached.

Mr Chopsticks became very ill afterwards and none of his children could look after him because most of them had been sent to the countryside to be 're-educated by peasants'. In fact, some of his children were ashamed of being a capitalist's child and didn't want to contact him in that Red time.

About three months later, early on a dark winter's morning, Mr Chopsticks heard a noise at the door. He got up, opened the door, and was shocked by what he saw: his cat, Mimi, lay there bony and dirty, with dying eyes. Mr Chopsticks couldn't save her; she died a few hours later. He couldn't bring himself to bury her, so he stayed with her cold body for many days, holding her and stroking her again and again. Suddenly he found something in her hair and feet: pieces of dry rice straw, boat lacquer with fish smell, and corn dust.

Where had she been? Mr Chopsticks lived in Nanjing, a city near the Yangtse river, but not on the north side where there were rice fields. How was this possible? Had she been taken to the other side of the river and back by boat? He sent a telegram to his seven children to say he was dying and that he wanted to see them. He told them the only thing he wanted to know before he died was where Mimi had been. His children held a meeting and made a plan: they would retrace Mimi's journey home.

At first they couldn't find any information. But when people on the north bank of the river heard about the 'cat hunt', many people who knew Mr Chopsticks joined the search because he had helped them in the past when they were in difficulty, or short of money, or jobless, or their houses had flooded. A fisherman's son said he had heard about Mimi from a boat factory worker. One day he saw a cat with a name tag of Mr Chopsticks' hidden in a bale of rice straw on his way home from the factory. He had heard his family talking about Mr Chopsticks' cat, so he took her back home. His mother said the cat was very ill and needed treatment before she could go home, so she fed her with rice liquid every day. But the cat looked very unhappy all the time. After two weeks, the family, worried that Mimi would soon die, gave her to the owner of the river ferry to take her back across the river. The worker didn't know what had happened next, but he gave the name of the ferryman.

Mr Chopsticks' children went to talk to the ferryman, who

looked very guilty. He told them: 'I had no idea how to look after a cat. It was cold, so I thought we should put her near the engine stove. Then she disappeared. I didn't worry about it because the boat was still on the river, but then someone shouted: 'Catch that cat! It stole my food!' I had forgotten to feed her! I ran out of the engine room and tried very hard to find her. But I couldn't. I'm so sorry.'

How had Mimi got off the boat and back home from the river bank to the city centre, full of cars and people? No one could find out.

But the next Chinese new year was the first time all Mr Chopsticks' children had spent new year with their father for a long time. They talked about Mimi's journey and their search, and their faces were full of respect. They were proud to be Mr Chopsticks' children.

Mr Chopsticks is my grandfather; I read this story in his diary. He wrote: 'I have got back my children, my love and my family, all from Mimi's journey home.'

30th April 2004

They move millions to a new town, replant entire mountains – the Chinese are amazing

'Is it chicken?' an editor from Portugal asked. 'No, it's fish cooked in wine,' answered the waitress. 'Is it fish,' asked an Italian agent, pointing to another dish. 'No, it's steamed pork.' 'Is it meat?' asked a Norwegian publisher. 'No, it's tofu . . .'

There were endless such questions from my 14 western friends on the first day of our trip to Beijing. We were there as part of a tour called 'Open Your Eyes to China Today', and although they 'knew' China from anecdotes, guides and history books, none of them had been before.

'I am naming the world all over again,' said a French editor. Despite being Chinese, I felt the same.

'Is that really the Beijing hotel – the famous party hotel,' I asked my Chinese guide two days later.

A five-star hotel, located in central Beijing next to Tiananmen Square and Wang-Fu-Jing high street, it used be the largest and best in town. It was also the tallest building in China and, before 1990, every Chinese person visiting Beijing had their photo taken in front of it. I remember the first time I looked up at it, in 1984, and what people were saying: 'Look, look, there are some golden hair and black faces in it.' 'One, two, three . . . oh, my God, there are 18 stores.' 'I heard only chairman Mao's guests can stay there.' 'Come on, we're in the queue. Get out if you've taken your picture.' 'Keep away from the front gate. Go away.'

Now I have returned and can actually stay in it with my western friends, even though none of us is a guest of Mao Ze Dong or Deng Xiaoping or Jiang Zemin. Some of the voices are still the same, though. A crowd of farmers, peasants and guards stands in front of the building. 'What a busy hotel,' they say. 'A real party hotel.'

The following morning, when my friends went to visit the Forbidden City and my room was being cleaned, I could not get a coffee because all three cafes were being used for government conferences. There was no space for my computer in the business centre – there was not even a chair to sit on while I waited for my room.

I went back to reception. 'Why do you offer rooms for tours if you can't accommodate them?'

'We need to make a living,' answered a manager, smiling nicely. I supposed she was familiar with this question. 'But how about those staying here,' asked another displaced guest.

'Sorry about this. In China, the words of our leaders and bosses are law, and we can't go against them. This is the Beijing Hotel.' Her voice was soft and proud.

'Corrupt,' said a Chinese woman in her 40s, who was standing behind me. She wore a business suit and carried an armful of files. 'What? Are you talking to me?' I turned to her.

'I'm talking to myself. I hate those corrupt people.' She was looking at the crowded meeting areas.

'Why? Do you know them?'

'Have you seen anyone leave those meeting halls with empty hands?' She still didn't look at me.

'No, but they might be carrying business files.' I really didn't want my enjoyment of the hotel to be destroyed by her hatred.

'Are you really Chinese?' And finally she looked at me, sharply.

'Is this the Great Wall?' a British editor, holding her guidebook, asked our Chinese tour guide. 'In my book this area is rocky and barren, but look, it's so green.' She showed a page to him.

'Oh, your book must be old. See? It's published in 2000, it's too old. Those are trees planted in the past few years.'

'All of them are new trees?' More loud voices, as we were joined by the Australian and American editors.

'Yes. What's wrong with them?' I could see that the guide didn't understand why these westerners were so surprised.

'How many people and how long did it take to cover so many mountains with trees?'

'It happened in just the past few years, after we were warned that Beijing could be buried in dust blowing from the north.'

'I see, but this is such a huge area.' My western friend still couldn't believe it.

'We are Chinese. We can move 30 million people from their poor old houses to the new buildings of our largest city, Chong-Qing, in just seven years, why can't we cover a few mountains with trees?'

In fact, I'm not surprised westerners who know about Beijing should question whether the trees and flowers in this green and colourful capital are real – they often used to be made of plastic.

11th June 2004

Twenty years after I first heard of it, I found myself scouring a Chinese street for a HongDu-Dou

She was standing there quietly, with some wild flowers. It was 1984, and many city-dwelling Chinese could offer only plastic beauty instead of paying the price of time and water for real plants. Her eyes followed some colourful foreigners, then lit on me, the first Chinese who had come to buy flowers in the seven years she had been selling them.

'How much is a bunch?' I had never bought real flowers before.

'Five fen [half a penny].'

'Is it the same price for those *Lao-wai* [foreigners]?' I could not believe she would stand there all day just for this 'between-the-teeth money'. I also knew lots of people charged those big-nosed, golden-haired foreigners 'heaven price'.

'Why should I sell to them at a different price? They love flowers just the same.'

'They really should be worth more, they are so pretty,' I said.

'I know. This is why I pick them up before they can be destroyed.'

'Destroyed?'

'They are digging to open up the Terracotta Warriors of the Qin dynasty, and so much is being destroyed. These beauties are gifts from heaven. Have you been to see the Warriors? You have to pray and protect yourself afterwards. I see you love flowers, which is why I tell you, I cannot let you be punished.'

'Punished? By what?'

'This is not allowed to be said, but every local knows it. The

Terracotta Warriors were discovered in 1974, then in 1975 the government decided to open it. Do you remember 1976? We lost our three heads: chairman Mao, prime minister Zhou Enlai, the head of the military, Zhu De – and there was the Tang-Shan earthquake with 300,000 lives lost.'

I was shocked. It was true that all these things had happened.

'How should I pray and protect myself?' I turned to her for help.

'Don't be frightened if you haven't done anything terrible. Get some incense to burn, then pray as the smoke goes up to heaven.'

'That's it?'

'That's it, if you are not guilty of any misdeed.'

I thanked her, bought 10 bunches of her wild flowers, then left.

'Wait,' she called after me. 'You should try to get a *HongDu-Dou.*'

'What's that?'

She shook her head. 'It's such a pity. Our young girls have no idea about traditional beauty. You must know that piece of red silk children wear in the new year posters. Silly girl, it is very good for a woman to wear this in bed with her husband. You should get one, even though you are young, because it could be forgotten very soon if our life goes on changing in this way.'

The same day, I bought the best incense I could and prayed, but I couldn't find a *HongDu-Dou.* I was told it had disappeared a long time ago, in the Cultural Revolution.

Two weeks ago, I went back to Xi'an with my western friends on a publishing trip. It has improved so much that I couldn't be sure I had been there before. We were told that new empty highways have been built and thousands of trees planted, ready for the Beijing Olympic Games in 2008.

When I went back to the Terracotta Warriors, I couldn't find the woman with her wild flowers. There were hundreds of people selling man-made stuff for tourists, but nothing from nature.

I told my husband I wanted to find this *HongDu-Dou*, and he came with me, along the narrow, twisting street that runs beneath the old city walls. There was traditional local food, and children's clothes – tiger shoes, lion hats and cat-baby coats – but no *HongDu-Dou*. No one even knows what it is.

On my last day in Xi'an, we went back to that street and, finally, I found it on a tiny stall. The seller was a young girl; she was so happy and surprised when I bought all 30 of the *HongDu-Dou*s she had. 'What do you want them for?' she asked.

'For your happiness,' I said, 'and my 14 western friends, who will have them as traditional Chinese gifts from my Chinese heart.'

25th June 2004

The ghosts of Qing-Zang: When Xinran met a woman who had spent 30 years searching for her lost husband in Tibet, she was inspired to write her extraordinary story. But then her subject went missing, too . . .

In 1994, an old woman dressed in Tibetan clothes smelling strongly of animal skins, rancid milk and dung sat down opposite me in the town of Suzhou in China, and began to describe the 30 years she had spent searching for her husband on the Tibetan plateau. I was working as a journalist at the time and had made the four-hour journey by bus from Nanjing to interview her. Her name was Shu Wen. A listener to my radio programme had called me after meeting her by chance at a street stall: he had never heard me speak about women's lives in Tibet, and thought I would like to meet her. He was right: I found myself so caught up in her story that I forgot to ask her all the important questions. I was so absorbed by her descriptions of Tibet that I noticed only the rough skin on her trembling hands and the deep emptiness in her eyes. I failed to realise then how little I really understood about the Tibetan way of life; I wasn't to know that this was a story I could never walk away from.

'Why did you go there?' was one question I did manage to ask.

'For love,' she said. 'My husband was a doctor in the People's Liberation Army. His unit was sent to Tibet. Two months later, I was told he had been lost in action. We had been married for fewer than a hundred days. I refused to accept he was dead. The only thing I could think of was to go to Tibet myself and find him.'

I stared at her in disbelief. I could not imagine how a young woman at that time – 1958 – could have dreamed of going to a place as distant and terrifying as Tibet. She, too, was a doctor, and after he went missing she decided to join the army to go in search of him: it was her only way of travelling to Tibet.

When evening came, Shu Wen was only part of the way through her story. I suggested we share a hotel room for the night and continue our conversation the next day. She agreed in the same brief manner that she answered all my questions. When she wasn't caught up in telling me about her experiences, her voice was flat and curt; she spoke Chinese with a strong Tibetan accent. I longed to draw her out more, so that I could ask her all the questions I had been storing up during the day – but it was clear that she considered all talk for the day to be over.

I was worried that her large body might not fit into the narrow single bed in the hotel room. But before she took off her Tibetan robe, Shu Wen removed her possessions from it like a magician producing birds from a hat. From two inside pockets came books and money, and from pockets on the sleeve some little sheepskin pouches. From her right boot she took a knife, and from her left some maps of China. She reached inside the waist of her robe and brought out two large empty leather bags. Then she removed her long silk belt, which was hung with even more little leather bags and tools.

I watched with astonishment: her robe, it turned out, was also her luggage. It became her bed as well. She spread it over the bedstead as a mattress, placed the silk belt over the books and maps to make a pillow, and then stuffed all her possessions into the sleeves of the robe, with the exception of the knife. This rested on the pillow beside her. Then she lay down, tucked the cuffs of the sleeves under her pillow and covered her legs with the two leather bags. Both her body and her possessions were perfectly protected. Underneath the robe and all that luggage, she was tiny.

I don't think she noticed my amazement as I got into the other bed. I felt as if I had just experienced a tiny piece of Tibetan life, and I would experience more when I went to Qinghai the following year to try to understand what it was that Shu Wen had gone through. There I would witness the incredible ingenuity of the Tibetan people, who manage to live with so few resources. I would see stones piled up to mark directions, food hidden in the frozen ground to be collected later, wood stored under rocks for fuel. I would realise that the leather bags that Shu Wen had spread over her legs were designed to carry dried food such as barley flour and curd when travelling.

The next day Shu Wen finished her story, and we parted. It wasn't until two days later that I realised I hadn't even asked her the words for the clothes and ornaments she was wearing, let alone the names of the protagonists in her story. All I knew was her name, and that she was Chinese, not Tibetan as my friend had originally thought. I had no idea how to find her again.

I called the listener who had suggested I meet her, but he didn't know where she was either. 'We got talking over a bowl of rice soup. Yesterday she sent me a tin of green tea from the fermented rice seller as a thank-you, and she said she hoped Xinran might be able to tell her story and that all women in love might be inspired by it. Xinran, I really don't know where she has gone.' And that was why I had to write her story.

I had been to Tibet once before, on a journalistic assignment in 1984. It was a short, five-day trip to the east of the Qing-Zang highlands, which are populated by a mixture of Tibetans, Mongolians and Chinese. For the first time in my life, I experienced what it was like to live in silence. I heard hardly any conversation. The Tibetans I saw seemed to communicate almost entirely by body language. I had been overwhelmed by the altitude, the empty, awe-inspiring landscape, and the harsh living conditions. What would it have been like for a young Chinese woman travelling there over 30 years before?

I made the trip to Tibet again in 1995. I wanted to follow in Shu Wen's footsteps and see the things she had told me about: the mystical connection between humans and nature, colours and silence, yaks and vultures. She had told me stories about Ao-Bao and Mani stones, Buddhist prayers carved into great boulders high in the mountains. She had told me about sewing men and multicoloured wind-chime women. Because traditional clothes were made from leather and metal, and sewing them was physically hard work, clothes-making was, and still is, mostly done by men. Tibetan women, no matter how poor, set great store by their jewellery, and everywhere you go there is the sound of bells and chimes as they move.

I learned about sky burial and water burial. Only when women die of an illness are they buried in the ground; otherwise the body is cleaned, shaven and cut into a thousand pieces, to be eaten by the birds, sending the soul back to heaven. Children's bodies are returned to the water, their hands painted red to protect them from the gods. I found it hard to believe what Shu Wen told me until I saw it with my own eyes. It was all so very different from the life I live, and even the many books I have read.

And then, in order to tell her story as it should be told, I spent almost eight years talking to people in Tibet and China and reading more books. Before I started writing Sky Burial, I had no idea there were so many Tibetans living up in those highlands, all with very different customs, beliefs, lifestyles and languages.

After all this time and all this work, I still find it difficult to understand completely Shu Wen's life – what she did in the name of love, and how she went from being a 26-year-old Chinese doctor to becoming a Tibetan Buddhist. After 30 years, she did find out the truth about her husband. In many ways, I feel I am one of the readers of my own book, too – a reader who still has a lot of questions I wish she could answer. I can't and don't want to invent those answers without her.

I don't know whether I could have endured the things Shu Wen did. But I would like to think that I could if I had to, for the sake of love, whether as a lover, a daughter or a mother. One thing I do know, from writing my first book, *The Good Women of China*, is that many Chinese women also devoted their lives to their families and to love, and many have endured as much as Shu Wen.

I will go on trying, as I have for the past 10 years, to find Shu Wen. At the end of *Sky Burial* I have written her a letter, asking her where she is. Perhaps one day she will answer it.

9th July 2004

A late-night knock at the door – is it the return of the Cultural Revolution? No, it's kick-off time

Last week I started to really worry about the two men in my life, my husband and my son. They were watching the final of Euro 2004, and they were just too excited. I realised how important it is to keep pills to hand – you never know when someone's going to have a heart attack.

Personally, I can't understand why they get so involved in other people's battles, but I do know that football is a game that drives the Chinese mad, too, even though their 'footballs' tend to be shoes, or old melons, or bags stuffed with grass, stones or thick wooden branches.

The first time I really became aware of football was when I read a book about Chinese communist soldiers playing football with their prisoners in 1949: '. . . no one remembers who is the winner or loser of the war on either side, or in the crowded audiences. Everybody concentrates on the game, which follows the rules and is not complicated by any political thought. The ball is very old and broken but no one cares. They shout and cheer; they applaud each goal, whether it is struck by a friend or an enemy . . . pain has been forgotten, hatred has been forgiven.'

In the book, an old peasant woman passes and asks, 'What are they doing?'

'They are fighting,' someone says.

'Fighting? They are still battling with each other after so many deaths?' She is very upset.

'No, they are fighting for a ball, not each other.' An old man tries to calm her down.

'For a ball? Why? There are so many boys fighting for one broken ball? Poor children, when I get the money, I will buy them each a ball, so they don't need to fight any more.'

My second football experience came in 1986, when I was woken by knocking on the door and hurried voices outside one night. My first thought was that the Cultural Revolution had begun again. I was terrified: I couldn't forget the suffering I experienced as a child and often had nightmares about it.

'Open your door, it's late!' the voices ordered.

'Who are you all? What do you want at this time in the morning?' I asked as I put on my clothes.

'Open the door . . . it's late, hurry up!' They started to beg.

They were my friends. As soon as I opened the door, more than 10 of them rushed into my two-bedroom flat, which had one of the very few colour televisions in the area. I stood there, watching them fill my small living room and turn on the TV. Not one of them took the time to say hello.

After an hour and a half, my fridge had been emptied and my beautiful clean floor was covered in muddy footprints, rubbish, dirty glasses and bowls. It was a chance for me to see another side of some of my closest friends: they completely abandoned any semblance of gentlemanly behaviour.

That, of course, was the 1986 World Cup, when few Chinese had televisions or, indeed, enough room for large groups of people to watch TV together. The matches took place as early as 3am Chinese time.

A third football experience came late one night in 1996. Because my radio call-in programme was broadcast at midnight, I was always one of the last to leave the building. I used to dream that some day I would have other colleagues to share my listeners' stories with, so that I wouldn't end the evening feeling so drained, going home alone in the dark.

Through football, I fulfilled half this dream. I had finished the broadcast with a call from a drunk husband who had accidentally killed his wife with a broken beer bottle. It was hard to tear myself away from listening to his voice on the phone, from a hospital where his wife had died less than a hour before, where police were waiting to arrest him.

The lights were still on in most of the other offices, but the building was silent. I wondered whether there was another secret search going on, for 'political reasons'.

I was wrong. In fact, every room was occupied by male colleagues with tears in their eyes. I was moved, thinking they had all been listening to my radio interview with the emotional husband.

I sat there quietly, rather enjoying the sad, collective emotion. Telephones rang, but no one moved to answer them.

'OK,' I said finally. 'I have to go.' I had to get home for my son, who was being looked after by a 17-year-old nanny. 'What about you?'

'We have to stay,' someone said. 'That's the deal.'

'What deal?'

'Don't ask too many questions, OK? We had a deal before tonight's football match: if we lost, then no one could go home to sleep. We all have to stay here at the office to prepare for the next game.'

I didn't say a word.

Over the next few days, almost every one of these men's wives or girlfriends called my office.

'Is Xinran there?' they said. 'Is it true that my husband was at the office that night after the football match? He said you are an eyewitness – are you? Who else was there? What did they do? Why didn't anyone pick up the phone?'

If only women had a game that gave them such licence to shirk their domestic duties.

23rd July 2004

If it says 'made in China' on the label, most Chinese just don't want to know

In city markets across China you will hear the following: 'Look at this beautiful silk shirt, made in America.' 'Look at these, real leather shoes made in Japan.' 'Over here – the very best chocolate, made in England!' On a publisher's tour of China in April, my western friends asked me what it was that people were shouting. I never knew what to say. Equally, I found it hard to answer my teenage son PanPan's question last year in a Shanghai department store. A saleswoman showed us a frying pan which she claimed had been made in Italy and 'designed by the Great British Museum'.

'You mean the British Museum is making frying pans?' PanPan asked her. She was standing behind a demonstration table wearing a western wedding dress with a veil.

'Yes, young man,' she said, smiling, proud of her grasp of the international market. 'You would know that if you read Italian.'

PanPan turned to me. 'Mum,' he said, 'when did they move the British Museum to Italy? Have they really gone into the frying-pan business?'

I told him to be quiet, but I sympathised – I had heard similar things many times myself. I once tried to buy Chinese-made underwear in China, but again and again was told that the best kinds came from America.

Many of my Chinese friends have been disappointed with the gifts I have brought them from the UK – toy telephone boxes, little London taxis, all stamped underneath, 'made in

China'. While western shops are full of Chinese-made products, China is increasingly obsessed with all things western – shops, fast food, hotels, even art, literature and architecture.

'Where can we go for an authentic Chinese shopping experience?' someone asked me on the publisher's trip.

'Xi'an,' I suggested, 'or Jinzhou [a 1,000-year-old town in Hubei province] or Zhouzhuang [a small village in Jiangsu province].'

My Chinese friends asked me why anyone would want to go there, where the shops were full of old Chinese junk: why not the big, westernised shopping centres of Shanghai and Beijing?

But I think visitors to China really do want to see these places, the real China. Xi'an was the first Chinese city to open itself up to the ancient world, not under the 'open door' policy of the 1980s, but during the Tang dynasty, when Xi'an was the first stop on the Silk Road. For more than 2,000 years and over 11 dynasties, Xi'an was China's capital, playing a vital role in bridging the gap between east and west. Xian's famous terracotta warriors of the Qin dynasty, an army belonging to one of the first emperors of China, are regarded by many as the eighth wonder of the world.

When I told a friend, a successful Shanghai businesswoman, how much my western friends had enjoyed visiting the grand mosque in Xi'an, she found it hard to believe. 'What did they get out of that old place? Shanghai's restored Yu-Garden is far more interesting. Trees full of birdsong? They can get that in our Plants Park. Spirituality? We have much more education and culture in Shanghai.'

Another friend, a journalist, pointed at the label on her Chinese Tang dress, which said, 'made in China'. 'Look,' she said. 'This was made in China, but the label is in English.' Any Chinese woman who was unable to read English would assume it had been made in the west. 'Shouldn't the label be in Chinese, too?' she said. 'Isn't it strange? Some women even want to give birth while on holiday so that their children are born foreigners.' She looked sad. 'You know, almost everything good that is "made in China" has been taken from us since 1840 [the start of the opium wars], and now we are only interested in rubbish made in the west.'

I didn't want to share in her pessimism. 'But we have a better life than we did 20 years ago, don't we?'

'Yes. But how much of our culture and traditions do we have left? I am afraid it is too late for some things, and that we have paid too high a price in abandoning all things "made in China".'

'It's just change, isn't it? Why do you feel so sad?' I asked.

Later, I spoke to another friend, a well-known writer, and told her about this conversation. 'Don't worry,' she said. 'At least our hearts are made in China.'

6th August 2004

Chinese girls adopted by westerners highlight a vast cultural divide that must be bridged

Since writing about adopted Chinese girls in this column last year, I have become a builder. I am building a mothers' bridge for adoptive parents all over the world, after receiving hundreds of emails and letters from people who have adopted Chinese orphans, more than 99% of whom are girls.

I also got a response from educated, middle-class women in China (few ordinary Chinese women have access to British newspapers). They found it hard to understand how western people could be so open-minded. In China, we never question other people's family set-ups, we only observe. We definitely do not discuss divorce and adoption; these are very private matters.

So my Chinese friends are shocked. Why would they let everybody know their children are adopted, they ask? How can they admit to everyone that they can't have children of their own? I thought westerners cared more about privacy than we did? What will happen when these girls grow up and go to China?

I was saddened by this mutual misunderstanding. How could these girls' Chinese birth mothers fully understand that their babies were loved and cared for by western adoptive families? How would an adoptive mother react if her daughter were to someday meet her Chinese birth mother? Would these mothers be proud of their western adopted daughters, if the girls came back to see them?

In fact, many western adoptive families struggle with these cultural differences, too. I have a British friend who adopted a

Chinese daughter (she also has two biological sons). She tried as far as she could to give her daughter a Chinese upbringing: a 'Chinese' bedroom, painted a Chinese red with paper cuttings of Chinese characters on the wall (one of them meant for a wedding), and Chinese toys, most of them really for adults (binding shoes, a back-scratcher, a teapot, a traditional round fan, a Qi dress or cheong-sam, a statue of Buddha, a foot massage bench, even an old lady's hat). Once, the five-year-old said to me, 'I don't want to be Chinese because I get different toys from my friends.'

Some families have asked where they can find 'typical' Chinese products and clothes for their adopted daughters. But what do they mean by 'typical'? I don't think it's something you can buy from the shops, not even in China. Children grow like plants – while the shape and form of the branch and its leaves may be very far from the roots, there is still a connection, through which they get support and nourishment.

Psychologically, the most important thing for adopted Chinese children is to allow them to move freely between the two cultures, so that they can develop and make their own choices. For adoptive parents, one way of feeling a greater connection with Chinese culture is by helping other poor children there. This is the purpose of the charity I am setting up, Mothers' Bridge (www.motherbridge.org), which aims to support adoptive parents and children. In spite of our different feelings about privacy and family, I believe we all, in China and the west, have a capacity for love. I also want to be able to help adopted children find an answer to that question: 'Why didn't my Chinese mother want me?'

I'll end with this poem by an anonymous author, sent to me by an adoptive mother:

Once there were two women who never knew each other.
One you do not remember, the other you call Mother.
Two different lives shaped to make you one.
One became your guiding star; the other became your sun.
The first one gave you life, and the second taught you to live it.
The first gave you a need for love. The second was there to give it.
One gave you a nationality. The other gave you a name.
One gave you a talent. The other gave you aim.
One gave you emotions. The other calmed your fears.
One saw your first sweet smile. The other dried your tears.
One sought for you a home that she could not provide.
The other prayed for a child and her hope was not denied.
And now you ask me, through your tears,
The age-old question unanswered through the years.
Heredity or environment, which are you a product of?
Neither, my darling. Neither. Just two different kinds of Love.

20th August 2004

A couple of unforgettable chickens reinforced my faith in human kindness

My son PanPan, who has just turned 16, has travelled from London to the Chinese countryside to teach children, on work experience. I've been very worried but after speaking to him on the phone I feel more reassured. His voice was very grown-up. 'Don't worry, Mum. It's not as bad as you said. It's very hot, 39°C. I've been thinking of the two chicken stories you told me.'

Once, PanPan had asked me what the most unforgettable meals of my life had been. I told him there were two chickens that had stayed in my mind. The first, I ate in 1992. I was visiting a village near Hefei, the capital of An-Hui province, on a press trip to 'greet the forgotten peasants'.

I was sent to stay with a family for the night, a couple with three children. Their daily meal was bartered with two chicken eggs. Every day, they would exchange the eggs for a little rice, flour, oil and some vegetables. Obviously, they were in no position to feed a guest. I knew I'd rather go hungry than eat what little food they had.

Their house had mud walls and a grass roof. The mother said nothing to me by way of greeting, just, 'Here is your bed, you'll have to sleep with the girls.' Her daughters looked like frightened rabbits, crowded on to a wooden plank – their bed.

They were about seven, five and two and a half, and they were excited about my visit. They opened my handbag and took everything out. They asked lots of questions: what was face cream, what was a handkerchief for, what do you put in a wash bag?

Their mother shouted out to us from the yard: 'Time for dinner.' I followed the girls through the dark house to the kitchen, which was next to a tiny chicken coop. The girls cheered and I caught my breath: there was a cooked chicken on the little broken table.

'Don't just stand there – come and eat,' said the mother. She was still very frosty. 'Why have you killed your chicken,' I asked. 'Please don't say it was because of me.'

'Of course it's because of you! You've come a long way, and you are our guest. Just eat: we've nothing else to feed you.' She was cold and unsmiling, but I was, and still am, moved by her kindness.

Four years later, I returned to see the family. They had become rich under China's open-door policy, and I was given 20 chickens and 100 eggs to thank me for my visit. But I still think that chicken I ate in their yard was an unrepeatable experience. I don't know if there is anyone anywhere else who would give half her worldly goods to a dinner guest.

My second memorable chicken experience was the first meal I ate outside China, in London in 1997. My friend and I were hungry after a 12-hour flight. We went to a little restaurant near Great Portland Street tube station. We noticed that everyone was eating chicken, so we decided to do the same. But our English wasn't good enough to order. A very tall, very smiley waiter came to ask what we wanted: we pointed to other people's plates. He shook his head and waved his hands, saying: 'No, no.'

'Yes, you have, you can,' I said. 'We want to chicken.' My English was very basic.

'Look, look!' My friend, who speaks barely any English, pointed to the table next to us.

'OK, OK,' he said, trying to keep it simple. 'Tell. Me. Which. Part. Of. Chicken. Do. You. Want?'

I translated for my friend. She must have been starving because suddenly she stood up and pointed at her arms, saying 'Here!'

'No, no, we don't serve here, or here, or here!' The waiter patted his arms, head and both feet.

'OK. Here.' My poor friend had lost all self-consciousness: she was patting her bottom and shouting.

'No, no. We cannot give you only here.' The waiter patted his bottom too, and raised his voice. 'We have to serve you here and here, together.' His right hand moved from his bottom to his lower leg. By now, everybody in the restaurant had stopped eating to watch us.

Finally another man, who was shorter and seemed to be the boss, came and put a whole chicken on our table and said something we couldn't understand. But we had to eat before we started worrying about the cost or what it was he'd said. In the end, they only charged us for the legs and the wings, not the whole chicken.

I had told PanPan that these two chickens had inspired me to try to bridge the divide between the poor and the rich in China, between the west and China. They made me see that you can find kindness when you least expect it, no matter where you are.

3rd September 2004

A shocking tale in a New Zealand bookshop is a lesson that hate is an emotion best forgotten

New Zealand was the first of 22 countries I visited between 2002 and 2003 to promote my book *The Good Women of China*. As well as a busy schedule and a lot of media interviews, I was asked to give a talk at a women's bookshop in Auckland.

During the two and a half hours that I was there, talking and signing books, my attention constantly wandered from the white faces surrounding me to the face of a grey-haired Asian woman in her 70s. Her eyes looked as if they were full of loss and sadness. She stood apart from the crowd, not approaching me with a question or asking to have her book signed.

When I had finished signing books, I waited to see if she would come and speak to me. Finally she did, the last person to leave the bookshop. In a quiet voice, she asked, 'Would you like to listen to the story of my life, which I have kept secret for 60 years?'

I could hardly say I did not have the time.

She told her story almost without pause. 'I went to China with my parents when I was five years old in the 1940s. My father was a commander in the Japanese army. He showed me how he murdered the Chinese, so that I would grow up with 'a man's heart'. He never allowed my mother to hide me from this violence. Afterwards, the Chinese army came looking for him. He escaped, but they got my mother instead and killed her in front of me. I was six.

'I was saved by a poor old Chinese peasant. He took me to his home town, a small village near the Great Wall, where I was hidden and brought up by the whole village, by each family in turn, living in each of their houses. Until the 1950s I almost forgot where I came from; all I had was a memory of murder.

'One day my Chinese father, the old peasant, said I should go back to my homeland, Japan. I was a teenager by then. Two months later, I was sent to the city with two men from the village. They handed me and a golden ring over to a very tall man, without saying anything. It seemed a deal had already been struck, and I didn't say anything either. After all the years of murder and hiding, I knew when to keep quiet.

'I arrived in Japan with no family. I had no idea where my father was, whether he was alive or dead, nor did I know how to speak the language. With the few words that I managed to pick up, I tried to ask people what had happened between Japan and China, but no one wanted to talk about the war. Still, in the home of almost every family there was a photograph of a dead relative with a candle in front of it, and that nearly broke my heart. I could not sleep for thinking about all the violence and murder.

'I missed my parents, as well as the Chinese peasant who had given me a second life. The relatives whom I managed to trace said that I was mad and should leave Japan because it was so full of terrible memories.

'So here I am. The country is different, the people are different, but in my heart, in my mind, nothing has changed. You cannot rid yourself of the memory of all that blood.

'I watched you on television this morning. When you said that the Japanese and the Germans, like the Chinese, have the same difficult pasts, because of the war and because of the Cultural Revolution, I thought you would be able to understand my life.'

I was stunned that the woman could recount such a shocking

story in such a gentle voice. 'Have you ever gone back to that village in China?' I asked her.

'No,' she said. 'How could I? How could I, the daughter of a murderer, ask anything of the Chinese?'

'Do you hate the Chinese? They killed your mother.'

'No. My father killed them, too, so we're equal. I think in some ways I am half Chinese.'

'I think you are right,' I said to her. 'We should leave hatred in the past: love and hope are for the future.'

She left the bookshop quietly, smiling slightly, but her stormy life story stuck in my mind long after the book tour ended. I am now going back to New Zealand for a second book tour (this time for my novel *Sky Burial*), and I find that the old woman's story is inextricably linked in my mind with this country.

I hope I will see her again.

17th September 2004

The young do not understand the madness and pain of the Cultural Revolution

Last month a friend asked me how much I really knew about China's past, even the recent past – just 20 years ago. Had I read any Chinese books about the Cultural Revolution, for instance? He found it hard to believe that China could take an objective look at its Red Period while the generation that lived through it is still alive. I told him I had read two books on the subject in Chinese, published in China, two months ago. One of them was *Part One: A Hundred People's Memories of the Cultural Revolution* by Feng Ji Cai; the other was *The Past Does Not Disappear Like Smoke* by Yi-He Zhang.

As someone who experienced this moment in history, these two books brought back such bitter, painful memories that – even though I was busy promoting my novel *Sky Burial* and setting up my new charity, Mothers' Bridge – I just couldn't sleep.

One of the stories in *Part One* was that of a woman who had killed her father with her own hands. She had tried to save him – an elderly academic – from the continual harassment of the Red Guards, but her parents had persuaded her to kill them both, one after the other. She killed her father, but there was not time to kill her mother: the Red Guards discovered that the family was trying to commit suicide. So she hugged her mother to her and they jumped from a fourth floor window. She survived but her mother died a few days later. She was charged with murder, and spent more than 20 years in jail. Her memories of her parents were very confused, she told the book's author, and although she ate three meals and went to sleep and got up every day, she hardly felt alive.

I completely understand these feelings of being dead and alive at the same time, and of having mixed emotions towards your parents. I was seven and a half when the Cultural Revolution took place and I, too, behaved as I thought a 'good daughter' should. My father was in prison and I wrote him a sentence in blood pricked from my finger. It said, 'You must repay the blood of the Chinese people!' I believed what I was told – that my father's family had helped the British drink Chinese blood as if it were red wine (my grandfather worked for the British company GEC for more than 30 years). This letter was stuck on the wall next to the meal table in his prison cell. I never talked to my father about this; I knew I could never erase the letter from either of our memories.

In one chapter of the other book I read, *The Past Does Not Disappear Like Smoke*, there is a story about an educated westernised family during the Cultural Revolution. A mother and her daughter try to live as if nothing has changed: they wear beautiful clothes, use the best china, listen to English radio. Soon, though, to keep the Red Guards from these things, they decide they must destroy everything. I know about this; I saw it, too – my skirts, my books, my toys, my beloved doll, all burned and destroyed at the same time. The Cultural Revolution was a mad, unbelievable, and unforgettably painful moment in the lives of so many Chinese people.

But I was sad to read, at the end of Feng Ji Cai's book, that when he went to interview young Chinese men and women about their feelings toward the Cultural Revolution, most of them had no idea what he was talking about. Some of them even asked why he would make these things up. Others said that China should have another revolution so that they could get out of exams; they couldn't believe that their parents had been so stupid as to sign up to Mao.

Perhaps I should not have been surprised by this: I have been asked the same questions by young Chinese ever since my book *The Good Women of China* was published two years ago. They, too, find it hard to believe that these things happened within the lives of the older generation.

China needs people like these two writers, Feng and Zhang, who are prepared to dig for the truth and to uncover painful facts. We need them so that a younger generation of Chinese can know how brave their parents were, and how much they owe them.

These books may not be 100% factual but, as Feng says, he has to protect the people who have told their stories, changing names, places, dates and other details. These people have suffered too much already to have their lives overturned again.

1st October 2004

My friends in China ask me to look out for their visiting children – but I have to draw the line somewhere

Every autumn since I moved to London seven years ago, I have exactly the same phone conversation with my friends in China – parents whose children are coming to study at universities in the UK and Europe. I would love to tape them, but of course, I haven't been able to persuade anyone. The conversations usually go something like this (me speaking):

'Yes, you can buy duvets and pillows in London. Britain is a developed country; you can get anything you want from the shops here. Yes, even soya sauce and vinegar. In fact, there are at least 10 different kinds of vinegar in the supermarket. Chinese vinegar? Yes, you can get that from the smaller Chinese shops. Fresh vegetables? Not always directly from a farmers' market, but still very good. Live fish? No, you can only get dead fish. The law doesn't allow people to sell live fish. I know, I know what they say – that live, jumping fish is much better for your health . . . Is it expensive? Absolutely. London might be one of the great cultural centres of the world, but it is also one of the most expensive cities on the planet. But you can't let your daughter carry everything with her from China . . .'

Then, the daughter will arrive with three huge suitcases, a rucksack and an enormous handbag. When I picked one girl up from the airport, the taxi driver asked me where everyone else was, the owners of all the other bags.

In the course of two years' study, this girl received further supplies from a friend of her father's, who came to London on business several times a year.

Before she went back to China last year, she shipped home two 50kg boxes of clothes, and left a number of brand-new, never-been-used things in my flat: a set of kitchen utensils; a rice cooker; 11 bags of cooking sauce (each of them big enough to cook for 20 people); three big bags of dried mushrooms; 12 bags of dried seaweed; 24 bags of instant soup; 16 bags of dried fish; 12 pairs of chopsticks; six food storage boxes; 22 bars of soap; four bottles of face cream; five bottles of shower gel; four new bath towels; four tubes of toothpaste; six bottles of body lotion; two mirrors; two handbags; 32 pens; 200 envelopes; eight hardback notebooks; three pads of paper . . . I'm going to have to stop there, before I run out of room. All of these things her parents would have bought for her in China.

This year, I have been talking to the mother of another girl:

'Is the beef safe to eat? Of course it is. Mad cows? Yes, there was a problem a couple of years ago. You've heard a lot of people died of mad-cow disease in England last year – where did you hear that? I read a British newspaper every day, and I've heard nothing about it. You think I'm being deceived by the British media? Come on, we have a proper legal system here. You think Britain is full of terrorists? That's not true. I am here and I don't see that people are living in fear in the way we did in China. Don't send your son to England if you are so worried. Really? He can't get a good job in Shanghai without a western qualification?

'OK, I will try my best to help him. But I won't be able to cook for him and look out for him in the way you would. Yes, of course I know how you feel, I am the mother of a son myself, you know that. But I think the best thing for our sons is to help them to be independent as soon as possible. They can't live under their mother's wings their whole lives. It's not a question of it being the western way of life, and I don't think we should let our children lose sight of their Chinese identity either – we just need to think beyond what's traditional.'

She obviously didn't think I knew what was best for her son. She called me soon after he arrived in London. 'Xinran,' she said, 'I don't care what you think is good for your son. Right now my son needs you to help him unpack! Can you please make sure he knows how to hang his clothes in the wardrobe? You'd be doing me a big favour.'

I couldn't believe it when her son opened up one of his two huge suitcases and took out pages of instructions on 'how to hang clothes', 'how to make a bed' and 'what goes where in your underwear drawer'.

'How did you manage when you were at university in China?' I asked him.

'My mother visited my dormitory every week.'

If we want our children to grow up and enjoy their own separate lives, we have to let them go a little.

15th October 2004

Eat them, catch them, or look at them in an aquarium. But what fish are really best for is explaining life

'Why are you so different when you're in the media?' PanPan, my son, asked me once. I thought it was too complicated to explain to him, a 16-year-old student, the idea that, 'Life looks different through different eyes.' So I told him: 'Your mum in the media is like a piece of fish served on a dish at the dinner table, after it's been chopped up and cooked by the chef. It is still called fish, but it is not a fish that can swim. So your real mum is the one with a head, a tail and bones, living in the water.'

'Why do you always use fish to illustrate your point?' he said. Why? I had never thought about this . . . I have to say that fish have always meant more to me than a food or an animal, or a work of art.

I first learned that a lie could be kind and beautiful from a book called *My Mum Likes to Eat Fish Heads*. In it, a university student finishes his first year of studying in the city, and wants to go back to see his parents, who are fishermen, in their tiny village. He tries to remember what his mother likes, but all he can think of is fish heads, because he has never heard his mother say she likes anything at all. When the family has fish dishes, she always says that she likes the head. So the student buys two cooked fish heads from a city restaurant for her.

When he arrives home, his mother has just finished her supper and is clearing the table, while his father is having his meal at work. The student is just reaching into his bag for the two cooked fish heads, when he sees, to his surprise, his mother throwing fish heads into a bin.

'Mum, don't you like fish heads any more?' he asks.

'My silly boy, nobody likes the bony fish head,' she says.

'But, when I was at home, you always told me you liked them and you showed me how much you enjoyed those bony fish heads,' he says.

The old mother looks at her big, tall son: 'I knew you were such a kind boy and wanted your mother to have the best piece of fish, so I lied. You needed it to grow up . . . a mother likes to lie for the love of her family.'

I used this beautiful lie to my English husband, who loves fish, while my son doesn't eat fish at all. One day, we were having dinner with my Chinese friends in a seafood restaurant in San Francisco. When the dish arrived, my husband immediately cut off the fish head and put it on my plate. My friends were so shocked, and asked me in Chinese: 'Are you sure this Englishman loves you? How could he give you that bony fish head in front of us!'

I learned how Chinese women are viewed in men's eyes from a toast that men used to make at the table in China: it describes how different women look like different fish. Let me get it for you from my first book, *The Good Women of China*. 'Mistresses are swordfish – tasty but with sharp bones; personal secretaries are carp – the longer you "stew" them, the more flavour they have; other men's wives are Japanese puffer fish – trying a mouthful could be the end of you, but risking death is a source of pride; men's own wives are salt cod – they will keep a long time. When there is no other food, salt cod is cheap and convenient, and makes a meal with rice.'

During my book tour, readers from different countries told me this toast would have suited their men as well.

When people ask me why I am lucky enough to have so many good friends and opportunities in my life, I answer that it is because I know a Chinese saying: you can't keep a fish alive in completely clean water. When something happens to me, I like to analyse why and what for; which is the fish, which is the water – and what do I want. If I want the fish that is happy in that dirty water, I try to live with the dirty water; if I need very clean water for something else, I have to give up the fish.

There are so many analogies, I don't think I could ever get away from the influence of fish in my life. My mother often mentions fish when we talk on the phone. When we spoke to each other on Chinese National Day – October 1 – she told me: 'Try to cook some duck this month, before they start eating mud and grass, and they still taste good from the insects they have eaten in the early autumn. Don't forget to cook some fish head soup with tofu – it's good for your health in autumn. And add some green leaves after you have removed the fish bones.'

29th October 2004

I used to think there were no good Chinese men, until a brief encounter at Paddington station

Since my book *The Good Women of China* was published, I've been asked many times why I haven't written a book about the good men of China. I've always said I'm not qualified; my excuse is that only a man could write such a book. But there is another reason – one I never tell people, but which is always at the back of my mind. My own experiences of China have left me with the feeling that there just aren't that many good men, at least not by the standards of modern civilised society.

I have little memory of either of my grandfathers. One of them died when I was little, and the other I barely knew. I got to know him when he was in his 80s through reading his diary, which was full of military history but contained little about his family – though he did write of his reservations about marrying a woman with big feet. In the end, he said, he didn't mind her feet too much as they made her stronger and better able to help him in his work. I read the diary again and again, trying to find something romantic about my grandmother, to whom he was married for 50 years, but there was nothing.

My father acted as both a politician and a manager in his children's lives. Whenever my younger brother or I visited him there was one family ritual we had to observe, and which never changed. He would order us to make tea for him, then sit down and listen to him: if we didn't follow what he said closely he would dismiss us as 'uneducated'. He asked us only about our work and our political beliefs (which had to be the same as his). There were no questions about our emotions, our friends. Then he would tell us to go home and work hard for the Party.

He would complain that my mother spent 30 minutes shopping at the farmers' market every day: 'I am an old man. I shouldn't be left alone.' No mention of the fact that his wife, who served 40 years in the army, was married to him for 50, and brought him three meals a day, was an old woman, too.

My brother is the father of a 14-year-old girl and the husband of a lovely, shy woman. Whenever I speak to him on the phone, he tells me just the bare minimum about family life. If I press him, he gets annoyed. 'My dear sister,' he'll say, 'you live a comfortable life in the developed world. I am struggling here in the *developing* world. I don't have time to worry about what people think, or what is going through women's minds. I am too busy to be the sort of husband and father you would like me to be.' I apologised for him to his wife, but she said in her quiet, powerful voice, 'There is nothing to apologise for. Like every working-class family, we haven't got the money to spend time together relaxing and being "romantic". If you want to see people living romantic lives in China, you have to go to the cinema.'

My niece takes a different view. 'My father doesn't need to work so hard,' she says. 'It's just an excuse so that he can go out drinking with his friends – and maybe other women, too. That is a man's life. Everyone at school knows that.'

Recently, two men upset my theory that there are few good men in China – all in the space of five hours. First, I was standing under the departure boards at Paddington station, trying to work out when the next train to Bristol left, holding a cup of coffee. The cup was so big that I couldn't reach the espresso at the bottom of it. I tipped the cup higher and higher, but still there didn't seem to be anything coming out.

Someone shouted at me, but I ignored them (this was London, after all). Then a Chinese man rushed up to me, took the cup from my hand and shouted: 'You silly woman – just look at your clothes!' I was stunned, but even more embarrassed when I looked down: my top and my beautiful silk trousers were completely soaked in coffee.

The man was angry: 'I can't understand how these cold-blooded westerners can stand there watching you pour coffee all over yourself and not say anything. I guess we're just very different cultures.' I thanked him, though I disagreed that we were so different.

Four hours later, at the end of my book reading in Bristol, a Chinese man asked me what men could do to change or improve life for Chinese women. I was touched by his question; it is rare that I hear from Chinese men.

So I guess I was wrong about the good men of China. If there were none, how would so many good women of China have grown up? The two Chinese men I met last month have planted a new seed of hope.

26th November 2004

Adjusting to life in London means roast pork, girls in smelly clothes and automated phone operators

Last week I went to a 'green-tea party' with a group of Chinese women. They talked about the lives they lead in London, as they do every year: they said that meeting like this is their version of the western 'round robin' that people send at Christmas. The idea is that they share stories and ideas, but the reality is that they end up sharing a lot of complaints. But I found it all rather interesting and thought-provoking.

One woman, a former schoolteacher in China and a mother of two, could hardly wait to get started. She was fired up with the frustrations of moving house in Britain.

'We just bought a house,' she said, 'and I can't tell you how difficult it is – all the phone calls you have to make to get gas, water, a phone line, your furniture delivered, a parking permit . . . It drove me mad. You have to put up with all those automated phone operators, a string of multiple-choice questions, and lots of technical language before you hear a real human voice. If you're lucky you might get put through to an operator, but first you have to join a queue and listen to terrible music for an eternity. If you're unlucky, you go in circles before being put back to the main menu.

'Does life in the developed world mean going without human contact? I miss the old phone operators. I miss arguing with them the way I did in China 11 years ago. It was the only time you could speak without worrying about who you were talking to or who might hear you – so much more human than all these western voice machines.'

An older woman in her 70s, the mother of two restaurant owners, was annoyed about her Chinese church. 'I used to go to a very small church, and there we tried to help each other all the time. Now I go to a very big church, but everyone just sits around criticising each other and gossiping. If we don't care about our immediate neighbours, how can we love God?'

Another woman, a mother of three girls whose family owns several Chinese takeaways in London, found it hard to understand why her children had so many school holidays. 'How much can they learn when they have all these long holidays with no homework? There is no challenge, no pressure, and all the classes are much slower-moving than in China. The government doesn't seem to realise how lazy this new generation is. You can already see it on the streets: how many kids know how to look after themselves? How many girls care about dressing well? Some of them look like mobile rubbish bins in their dirty, smelly clothes. I don't want my daughters to turn out like that, but what can a Chinese mother do to resist this western life?'

An artist who was visiting her daughter in London said, 'I thought London was meant to be the cultural centre of the world, but the names of the streets, the squares, the buildings, people's names – even the menus – are so boring. They all seem to come from the Bible – St Peter's, St Paul's – or the royal family – Queen A, Queen B. There is nothing that tells you anything about the place itself, its history or how it came to be there; there is only royalty and religion.

'Take restaurant menus, which are just a list of different animals' names and how they have been cooked. In China, the names on a menu refer to local history, folklore, or poetry; you would never see a dish described as crudely as "roast pork", for instance. Even in a tiny, shabby family restaurant in the country, you get very descriptive menus. Why does the west lean so much on its history, but never bring it into its daily life and language?'

One woman didn't speak unless she was spoken to, and even then she said just one sentence in a quiet voice: 'I've started shopping in Knightsbridge rather than Oxford Street this year.'

Everyone congratulated her, but I had no idea what the significance of this was. Someone explained. Apparently, when she came to London 15 years ago she used to tell everyone you could buy two chickens for £1.99 at the market behind Brixton station. Then she graduated to supermarkets, and then to delicatessens and boutiques. As her wealth increased, so her choice of shopping destination evolved. It was a map of the course of her life. A Chinese saying came to mind: 'One's voice becomes more distant as one's price becomes higher.'

10th December 2004

How China has embraced all the bright lights and overindulgence of a very merry Craze Mass

'Have you started Christmas shopping?' My friends have been asking me this since early November, when my head was still filled with Zhong Qiu Jie, the Chinese mid-autumn festival. Six weeks until God's birthday is a long way to go, I thought.

'Did you do Christmas shopping when you were in China before 1997?' I did some, but it would be hard to call it Christmas shopping when you compare it to the hundreds and thousands of shopping bags that block the London streets. I was already too old for Christmas shopping, which in most Chinese eyes was considered a western romantic bit of fun for the young.

In fact, the first Christmas things after 'open policy' was introduced came not from those big department stores where staff were trying to change their manner from very officious to more encouraging and commercial; nor from 'the foreigners' friendship shops', which sold only to foreign diplomats and top officials, who paid in dollars. At that time most Christmas things were sold in the markets full of '*xiao shang, xiao faner*' – hucksters shouting 'the best from western Craze Mass'.

I once asked a market trader in Nanjing, a woman in her 60s wearing a red beret, 'What is Christmas? What's it for?'

'That is the date for USA God! You see my hat, this is their Craze Mass hat, westerners like the colour red . . . I did wonder if that was true after everybody said capitalists like black; but as you know, those rich capitalists are very colourful. Money and wealth bring colour to human lives . . . come on, buy one, forget your age. . . we have missed out on a lot.' I bought my first ever Christmas tree from her. It was made from paper, was no bigger than my hand and had sesame seed-size stars.

I didn't think too much about how logical her theory on money and colour was, but afterwards I could see it not only in the festival celebrations but in China's improved daily life. Between the 50s and 80s Chinese people wore a uniform of blue, grey and military green – but not black as that is too capitalist and signifies bad luck.

Christmas, which has become a big thing in the cities over the past few years, has brightened up China in the winter. I recently saw a photo of a Chinese family's Christmas Eve in Tianjing, a harbour city near Beijing. Six family members – three grandparents, two parents and one daughter – were all standing with a huge plastic Father Christmas next to their dining table; you could see the colourful lights and beautiful flashing curtains behind them.

I have to say, in my parents' photos, before they were burned by the red guards, I never saw such rich colours, even though they painted the colours on to black and white photos. But they never painted that much colour in.

Last year I did my Christmas shopping in China. The city streets were filled with red, green and gold – the colours dancing and flashing; shop staff waved streamers, giftboxes and angels; in the bookstores, you could see lines of coloured lights jumping up and down to the music. It is like this for the whole of December.

My family and I were on Hainan Island for Christmas last year. We stayed in a western hotel in HaiKou, the capital of Hainan. There was an unbelievably huge choice of seafood for the guests on Christmas Eve, masses of food, more than 10 cooks performing, innumerable waiters, hundreds of diners, loud music, sweating dancing girls, shouting parents and crying children.

I could see my husband had completely given up on trying to hear anything, he was just enjoying his food. My son couldn't keep his eyes off the Chinese Christmas dresses. I felt so dizzy from all the moving colours. I needed more than a few days to recover from this rich feeling of overkill. But only the next morning a Chinese Father Christmas gave my 60-year-old husband a lot of sweets at breakfast.

'This is unfair!' a friend of mine shouted when she heard this story. 'In a restaurant in ChongQing, a city of 30 million people, Father Christmas came up to my son, who is just four years old, and presented him with the bill in a very big colourful bag – no sweets at all!'

14th January 2005

In 1976 an earthquake in China caused double the death toll of the tsunami. But no one talks of that

I was cooking in the kitchen on Boxing Day when my son PanPan ran over: 'Ten thousand people have died in a tsunami!' I could hardly believe it, and when I saw the aftermath of the disaster on television, I was shocked beyond belief: 10,000 lives swept away in a matter of seconds by a series of vast waves. Over the days, the death toll crept up to 150,000 and is still rising. Towns and villages were wiped off the map, entire communities swept away, and millions made homeless, then threatened by disease. I was deeply hurt as I saw children crying, orphaned by the disaster.

The word earthquake had reminded me of the one in Tang Shan – an industrial city near Beijing. That earthquake claimed up to 300,000 lives on a July morning in 1976, but how many people around the world knew? The question remains unanswered, but the event is still crystal clear in my mind.

One survivor once described to me the 14 days of misery that she had endured, watching helplessly as her daughter died in front of her. At 4am, Mrs Yang was woken by an earthquake so powerful it broke her apartment in half. She was lucky to have been in the safer half, but her young daughter had been in the other and had fallen four storeys into the rubble.

She made it down the collapsing stairs and began a search for her daughter. Amid the noise of chaos, the woman heard her daughter's cry – the lower half of her body was sandwiched between two reinforced-concrete slabs. Her husband had died a year before, her daughter was all she had, and she was not going to let go.

She tried hard and onlookers helped, but the task of lifting concrete was no job for bare hands. So they waited and waited until the soldiers arrived, but they could not do anything either, as they did not have the necessary equipment as the roads into the city had been destroyed.

All they could do was give the girl water and some food. And so they waited. They waited until more and more people gathered to sympathise, until her daughter's voice became more and more frail, until her mother's heart was torn to pieces. For 14 days and 14 nights, her mother stood by her, until the little girl gave up her last breath. For Mrs Yang, the grief was too much to bear.

But that was just one sorrowful story in the whole of Tang Shan. Anyone who has been there would have heard about how the earthquake showed mercy only to a few buildings left standing, how the rest collapsed, swallowing their inhabitants with them. Deep cracks in the earth jolted open, sleeping people fell into the rubble. Roads contorted, the city became inaccessible, aid could not get in. Soldiers and survivors dug with their hands to rescue the dying; people kept scrabbling at the debris even when their hands were gloved in blood, but only those near the surface were fortunate enough to be rescued.

Days went by and the trapped perished in their thousands, either crushed by the weight of the rubble or dying of starvation. It became increasingly important to dispose of the bodies, so soldiers were ordered to douse everything – bodies and debris – with petrol and burn it, in order to eliminate the threat of disease. But the mental damage was phenomenal. The soldiers involved, whom I interviewed in 1995, were still haunted by those memories after almost 20 years.

No one I have met in the west has ever mentioned the disaster of 1976. The Chinese government tried hard to conceal the event, thinking it could 'manage it on our own' and wanting to show the rest of the world that China was stronger than they imagined. That thought cost lives. At a point when every hand available was needed to help those people, China turned down the offer of international aid that might have saved so many more lives.

Money repaired the destruction caused, and the population was restored in a few generations, but even after 20 years when I interviewed some of the survivors, the memories of the earthquake were still there, and may never leave those mentally tormented minds.

Could we do more than giving international aid to the Asian survivors? Yes, they need the support for their hearts to keep them going for the years to come.

28th January 2005

Receiving a handwritten card in this age of computers is one of the great pleasures in life

More than a month has passed and some of my friends still haven't recovered from their exhausting Christmas work: writing dozens, or even hundreds, of cards (and always regretting it when someone is missed off the list), carrying heavy shopping bags, gift-wrapping, storing and preparing enough food to keep a big family going for at least three days, cleaning the house, digging out fresh ideas for the party; and all without the help of nannies and cleaners, who have gone on their Christmas break.

As a Chinese person living in the west, it is very simple for me to get away from such festivals, because the Chinese don't celebrate Christmas or Easter, just as the west doesn't have Spring and Middle-Autumn Moon festivals. But there is one thing at which we are much busier than westerners – writing cards for all those festivals. Last year I decided to store all the cards so that I could see and record all the differences in culture and language – and people's personalities as well.

On the last day of 2004 I counted up all the festival cards I had received during the year. I found that 273 were from westerners and 169 from Chinese. Most of the cards from westerners were similar: names and signatures with printed greetings on high-quality paper. Only about 30 have some handwritten scribble that is hard to read (on one of them I had to spend more than three minutes reading one sentence) and seven also contained family letters.

Chinese cards are much more varied in quality and languages

– English, traditional Chinese and simplified Chinese, and even some that were a mixture of three or more languages. But I could read their 10 sentences in three seconds.

My son asked me: 'Which is the best card you received in 2004?'

I didn't take a second to answer. 'Shenshen's Christmas card.'

Shenshen is studying theatre production and playwriting at Royal Holloway, University of London. She is the director of a show called *China Chopsticks* and works as a volunteer for the charity The Mothers' Bridge of Love (MBL). I was, and still am, touched by her Christmas card in four colours.

'I have nothing to give you as a material gift; I would like to write a letter to you in my handwriting as a present from my heart. As a poor student, this is the best way to get on with this expensive festival and with the one I respect and love.'

The first page is green. She told me why she likes green – it represents peace, life, creativity and her mother's character, all her supports in her lonely life in this strange country. The second page is orange, and she tells me how she is inspired and energised by love, warmth, westerners and MBL. The third is yellow, which gives Shenshen an impression of wisdom and her interests in the daily life of the very different cultures that she encounters: sometimes she can't help herself speaking Chinese to her non-Chinese classmates. On the last page, purple, there are a few greetings, with Shenshen's name written in calligraphy.

I always respect handwritten letters, and admire people who spend time writing to their family and friends on paper, in this age of uniform computer writing. I miss that time. I would like to read letters as if I touched the writers' hands and saw their personalities through their writing – they are never the same, as everyone is different in your life.

I don't know many Chinese mothers and children who spend

time writing to each other instead of talking on their mobile phones. Oh yes, I know emails have become a part of family conversation. But I am quite sure many mothers would still love to open their children's letters and cards and read hand-written words, even if some of them were damaged by rain or the author's tea or coffee.

My son, who writes to me every week in Chinese hand-writing, quietly heard Shenshen's story while I was doing my Christmas cooking, then said: 'Should I do one year's washing-up at home, mum, as a Christmas present for you?'

'Yes! No, wait, you are in boarding school and travel all the time on your holidays, don't you?'

At Christmas, I got a card in his very good Chinese hand-writing: 'Little money, big love, to Chinese children from PanPan,' with a £20 donation from his savings to MBL. And he had been doing washing-up all the time, as always.

11th February 2005

Victorious Egg Festival, Sexual Hooligans' Day? It was once hard to understand western festivals

In November 1989, my radio station had a directors' meeting to discuss which western festivals we could mention on air. The meeting was held by a director in his 50s who had become a news broadcaster at the age of 15, as he had been one of the few people who could speak Mandarin in the early 1950s when the station started out in Henan. At that time, most people knew only their own local dialect.

The first festival we discussed was Christmas, which in Chinese sounds like 'Victorious – Egg – Festival'. 'What does that mean? Victorious Idiot Festival? Or just use some eggs for a victory?' the senior director asked when he heard this word. We all laughed. In Chinese, any adjective plus the word egg means an idiot.

His anger quickly shut us up. 'Why are you all so happy to hear about western capitalist culture? This is a defeat for China. Should we laugh at losing our revolution? Are you crazy? Improvement is not about changing our communism into capitalism. Open policy is not about opening up to our enemy. Have you ever thought which side you are on? Have you forgotten our duty as a political tool? What we are doing is helping people to get more knowledge of the rest of the world . . . so that we can unite all the poor people in the world against bloody capitalists . . . Not give up our principles and duties.'

No one dared to laugh again. We never dreamed of saying no to a political leader, even one who was uneducated and lacking any knowledge of the outside world. We had all been formed into the same shape and colour – and political view – because we had been brought up with political propaganda. Everyone working in the media knew that rows could cause trouble: if you were lucky, you and your team would have your pay cut and the incident recorded in your personal file, which stays with you for life; otherwise, you could be sent to prison as an anti-revolutionary.

Therefore, the biggest western festival, Christmas, was struck from our radio station's 'open policy'. (By the time I left, in 1997, Christmas still had not been discussed on air.) The next festival to be brought up was Valentine's Day – 'Lovers' Day' in Chinese. 'You see why we say western society is rubbish. They are not only allowed love affairs but also give those sexual hooligans a date to celebrate. They should be sent to prison as they are here in China,' said the senior director.

Good Friday. We didn't know what to say about this religious holiday, so passed on. Easter in Chinese is pronounced 'God Resurrecting Festival'. 'No,' he said firmly. 'No way. Our great leader Chairman Mao hasn't risen again. How could we tell people that the western God has?'

He thought it was unfair that Mothers' Day came earlier in the year than Fathers' Day. 'Why is the west still such a matriarchal society, despite its development? OK, admittedly Chairman Mao said, "Women make up half the sky". So let Mothers' Day be . . . but don't make too much of it. Xinran's late-night programme should be enough. The important thing is that Mothers' Day shouldn't be made a bigger thing than Fathers' Day.'

Someone described Halloween as 'the day before All Saints' Day in the Christian calendar, when, according to tradition, you can expect to see ghosts and witches wandering about'. Our director sat looking at the ceiling, not saying a word. We all thought Halloween would be frowned on. No superstition allowed. The next day he came into my office and said: 'Xinran, you have read a lot. Is it true westerners can see ghosts and witches? My mother told me she had seen them as well. You won't let other people know what I just said, will you?'

After a while he spoke again. 'How different we are to the west. Why so different? If their God can be born again, why not Chairman Mao?' Before he left, he told me he was going to borrow the only book at our radio station about western religions. Then he walked out, asking: 'Why do they name a festival after a victorious idiot?'

Fifteen Christmases have passed since then. Even people like me who have experienced the Cultural Revolution can hardly believe how Chinese lives have changed. 'Sexual Hooligans' Day' – or Valentine's Day – has become popular. I can't imagine how my old director, now in his 70s, is coping with the great speed with which China is changing.

25th February 2005

The west ruined our self-confidence years ago. Now, finally, we're getting it back

I can't tell you how happy I was – and still am – after leaving the Chinese embassy in London last week. The long queue, which snaked along the street and was full of people with different colour hair and eyes, reminded me of queuing in Beijing for a British visa back in 1997.

We – who all wanted to have a look at the world outside China for various reasons – were nervous, ignorant and frightened: none of us had ever been abroad, some had never even travelled within China. We hardly knew what the differences were between Britain and China, we knew nothing of Britain's religions, law, or social system, just that it was an 'old, dying capitalist country' built on centuries of plundering and the slave trade.

We were so scared by what the 'advisers' and 'immigration agents' had to say. They told us that the British never believe the Chinese, that they would test us with many difficult questions in English, they would call our work unit and check out every single part of our application documents. If just one person said 'don't know' when they were called up that could be recorded as a black mark on your personal file – which, since 1949, the government had kept on every member of the Chinese population. Then you would never be able to go abroad.

We viewed the world through our Chinese understanding. But, yes, we still wanted to take the risks because we thought we could have more career opportunities with a British degree or training. Most of us had done quite well in China, and were looking for new challenges in the west.

Eventually, I got in to the British embassy visa office: the waiting room was full of smartly dressed Chinese – who believed expensive clothes would show they were educated. Everybody was carrying huge files stuffed with endless certificates. They thought that the British officials valued membership of the communist party and party prizes as a mark of good judgment in China. Young people were madly practising their English.

The receptionist's cold voice called out numbers and warned people not to talk. I felt like a guilty woman awaiting sentence. My pride and confidence plummeted. I saw another empty room through a big window, where there were comfortable chairs and fewer people – westerners were talking and laughing there, neither nervous nor frightened. And no cold voice stopped their noisy chat.

I did not feel uncomfortable with what I saw as I was used to being made to think that 'foreigners were respectable'. I think that might stem from the Opium War in 1840 when westerners knocked down China's door with arms and opium, burning down our spirit and self-confidence. Even the Cultural Revolution, when we were taught that every western capitalist could be a spy, failed to dim that notion of foreign supremacy.

One woman I interviewed in China had been in jail for nine and half years: she had been arrested in 1969 for catching a thief – a foreigner – on a Beijing bus. At the police station she was asked: 'Why do you slander our foreign comrade? The people who come from capitalist countries do bad things in China as spies and thieves; this man comes from a socialist country. What you have done could damage our friendship.'

The poor woman, who had had her purse stolen, was then put into prison for 'attempting to destroy China's great image abroad'. After the 1980s, the west became God-like to many Chinese because of westerners' wealth, and freedom to do what they want. This is why I never dreamed that Chinese should take priority anywhere. But I felt it was really unfair that I, a Chinese passport-holder, had to queue with foreigners at our own embassy. After all, most nationals have preferential treatment in their home embassies.

Last week, I could not and did not believe the sign on the wall: Chinese passport-holders can go to window 5 without queuing. Not until I heard a warm voice say: 'Please come to window number 5 if you are a Chinese passport-holder.'

Oh, thank you, Chinese embassy, you have made me feel better to be Chinese. I could see admiration in the eyes of those queueing in the Chinese visa office. Chinese people really need that after years and years of living with humiliation and discrimination.

11th March 2005

The gap between western and Chinese paintings is as vast as that between the two cultures

My husband loves art and has tried very hard to improve me. He likes to show me how one can understand what it is to be poor from viewing Celso Lagar's 'A Traveling Circle' and that women can comprehend the feeling of wartime defeat from Lotte Laserstien's 'After War'. He buys books, visits galleries and hangs artworks on every wall in our flat. However, I remain just as ignorant of western art works. I don't like to be overwhelmed by the details in western drawing and the western fullness of colour. I want to be allowed to imagine and experience the artists' feeling and thoughts in my own way, guided by the simple lines, economic use of colour and empty spaces in Chinese and Japanese paintings.

I want to share more with my husband, so I called our friend Lei Lei, a Chinese artist, who understands the painting of both our cultures and explores the differences in his work.

'Come to our house, we could talk about this during a meal, I will cook for you.' He spoke with the tone of a demanding Chinese man, but a man cooking for women is a western cultural phenomenon.

Lei Lei's house could be described as a gallery or an artist's workshop, but it is also a place full of Chinese culture. He welcomed us with western kisses and hugs, his wife Caroline appeared like a Chinese wife with apron and wet hands from the kitchen.

While Lei Lei cooked, he gave me my first art lesson. His knowledge was steeped in ancient Chinese philosophy – the root of Chinese art – but my level of knowledge was too poor to understand everything. As a naughty student would, I decided to go to the bathroom. The walls along the stairs were full of paintings. I liked almost every one. I realised that the ones I thought were Chinese were painted by Caroline, and others, which seemed clearly western, were by Lei Lei. How could Caroline understand Chinese culture so well and how could Lei Lei so successfully influence his western wife? This is exactly what Toby and I wanted to learn from them. This was much more important than all that academic knowledge.

On my return, the lesson changed to women's studies. Caroline told me the following story in Chinese: 'It was years ago, about 1990, when I came back from China. My feeling was that I had had enough of it. I felt the need to be truly English and reconnect with my own identity. It was about then that Lei Lei came into my life and it was almost as if I was punishing him for the hardships I had endured. For instance, he spoke in English most of the time when he could easily have spoken Chinese. In his quest to win my heart, he invited me and some old friends around for supper.

'When I arrived, he said to me: "I want you to serve the rice!" His voice was insistent. I shrugged and said it was fine. "I also want you to pour the tea," he added, in a similar commanding way. Throughout the meal I did as he asked. I spooned out the rice, I poured the tea and as I did so he paused in his conversation to check that his friends had noticed. I felt self-conscious. I noticed that every time I performed these tasks he rapped his knuckles on the table – as if reproaching me or demanding that I hurry up. As his guests went, I picked up my coat to leave myself. Lei Lei looked at me: "What's the matter?" I almost cried. "I am not your slave!"

'"I need to tell you a story," he said calmly. "Hundreds of

years ago there lived an emperor who was extremely good at chess. It seemed that no one was as good until one day a peasant was found who matched the emperor in ability, so the emperor could never get bored. There rose a small dilemma though, when both players would need to break for a meal or tea. If anyone dined with the emperor, no matter how informal the meal, they had to kowtow to him 100 times. This became extremely time-consuming and irritating. So the emperor came up with the idea of the peasant placing his index finger and the one adjacent to it on the table and rapping – like rapping one's fingers on the table as if you were demanding something in a restaurant in an extremely rude way."

'It transpired that by rapping on the table, Lei Lei was kowtowing to me 100 times. I never did discover the significance of my serving the rice and pouring the tea. But I have learned that however occasionally frustrating and confining it is to be with him I will never get bored.'

25th March 2005

How to bridge the gulf between Chinese and western painting

I asked my artist friend Lei Lei if there was a story that could explain the difference between western and Chinese painting. He gave me two. The first happened about 1,600 years ago, when the great artist Gu Kaizhi created 'The Picture of the Ode to Goddess Luo'. He brought the idea of Chinese spiritualism to art, where the inner emotion is revealed through figuration.

The painting referred to the great war of 200AD when China was on the verge of being divided up. Cao Cao had north China under his control. He had two sons: Pi, his arrogant and domineering older son, later became emperor; Zhi, the younger son, made his name as a gifted poet and scholar. Though Zhi never showed any interest in politics, Pi was always suspicious of him, looking for excuses to kill him.

The heroine of the story, Lady Zhen Luo, was the daughter-in-law of Cao's enemy. She was a legendary beauty and all three men in Cao's family fell in love with her. According to Luo, only one man deserved her favour: Zhi. However life laughs at people's expectations. After Cao won the war, Pi rushed into the enemy's palace, and kidnapped Luo. Luo was forced to marry Pi but died soon after. For Zhi, it was bad enough having his beloved become his sister-in-law, but then he was parted from her for ever. In this inconsolable pain, he created the 'Ode to Goddess Luo'.

The Ode was about a dream in which he met the Goddess of Luo River (the incarnation of Zhen Luo). They fell in love and had a magical time together. When morning came, the goddess reluctantly had to leave. Astride her dragon, she turned back and waved again and again, sad and dolorous.

Gu Kaizhi's painting was based on Zhi's Ode and emphasises the unspeakable plaintiveness between the lovers, especially in their eyes. This plays on the viewer's knowledge of literary anecdote. The idea of 'conveying the spirit' then became a principle in Chinese art and has been constantly developed and enriched by generations of painters.

The second story is about the man who brought western painting to China. Castiglione, 1688–1766, a Jesuit missionary and a good painter, entered China in 1715. His work was influenced by baroque art and chiaroscuro. He was made a court painter and later took part in designing Yuan Ming palace – the unmatchable palace that was ransacked and burned down by the British and French coalition troops in 1860, leaving just a few ruins on some desolate land outside Beijing.

When Castiglione painted the emperor's portrait, the emperor asked him: 'How come my face is half light, half dark?' Chinese painting never depicts the sun, nor shadows. Chinese started to draw the link 3,000 years ago between the sun and the son of heaven – the emperor. When they couldn't bear the emperor's harsh repression any longer, they cursed the sun.

Castiglione soon learned from Chinese art how to use lines and rhythm. Combining western figuration with Chinese spirit, he created a new style of painting. If it had been a Chinese artist who had painted the emperor's face half black, half white, he would have lost his job, if not his head.

8th April 2005

When Chinese art meets western culture, an inner world is revealed

After all my artist friend Lei Lei's stories of painting and art, I asked him whether he had worked out how to mix western and Chinese culture together in his paintings. As his answer, he took me to look at his work for a new exhibition.

They are a series of giant faces. You could describe them as large portraits, but I think they're setting out to go beyond the portrait into a larger, unified piece of art. Each piece will not only portray the face, brilliantly drawn in Chinese ink on rice paper (this is extraordinarily hard to do since you cannot rub out, or erase, or change the ink once it has been applied. It's much harder than oil painting or pastels. I tried once before: the ink ran away everywhere – where I didn't want – and the tablecloth was completely destroyed. And what did I paint? A flower that looked just like a broken umbrella!), it will also contain a message from the sitter about what visitors to the exhibition can learn from their lives.

The whole art work is modelled in the Chinese style, which is extremely ancient in its origins. The faces will also be emerging from a window of larger papers in front of a collage. I felt that Lei Lei had talked with those faces, those sitters, a lot, otherwise I couldn't imagine how he could draw them in so much detail and be so touched by their souls.

The idea that everyone's life is of value is significant, he said. Things aren't always how they seem. For instance, the woman in the chip shop probably lived through the world war. She may have lost a child. She may have found a child. I could see that

Lei Lei's explanation of his many points could run well into the early hours of the morning. I believe that woman is more aware of time than man: Caroline [Lei Lei's wife] mentioned that it was midnight already.

Before we said goodbye, I asked her about Lei Lei's exhibition. She is so proud of it and said: 'Finally, and far from least in importance, is the idea of combining ancient and modern concepts and ideas. In the ancient traditional Chinese markings – the writing on the image, and also at times calligraphy, and maybe at times the whole idea that everyone's life is an epic – this can be seen. I'm sure there must be some philosopher who came up with that one, or is it original?

'A last special thing that I think I like is that all the faces look as though they are peering through a giant door or window. The giant door or window is probably abstract and full of tensions, pulling our vision forwards and backwards and at the same time with the face itself. This blend of abstract with figurative is, I think, the last point of interest as well.'

Honestly, I have no idea how much I understand from a lesson of a few hours. From what Lei Lei has taught me, 'conveying the spirit' or 'spirit visualisation' means to reveal the inner emotion and hidden implication through ways of figuration; and combining the western figuration with Chinese taste and spirit. From Chinese paintings we can learn how to use lines and pay attention to their rhythm and charm, something that gradually created a new style of painting by Castiglione.

Certainly, I know that Chinese painters could not only use white, grey and black to draw colourful seasons, but also use very simple lines to inspire the imagination, so that different people could get different impressions from the same painting. It is a form of 'demarcated art' for everybody. Western paintings are much more 'official' – the light, colour and line, every detail has been dictated by careful drawing.

'Shut up!' I know, people might shout at me – I am, after all, someone who has had just a few hours' learning and dares to talk about great art and painting. I should know that no matter if it is western or eastern art, before you want to reach it you have to climb thousands of stairs.

It is hardly necessary for me to say that you all should have a look at Lei Lei's exhibition. You would be touched by the conversation between western and Chinese culture, stranger and friend, man and woman, life and death, face and soul.

Lei Lei's exhibition *Everyone's Life Is an Epic*
was at the Ashmolean Museum in Oxford
from 23 March until 17 July 2005

22nd April 2005

China is my homeland. But these days – in the bars, cafes, on the streets – I am lost in translation

When you are in Rome/China, do as the Romans/Chinese. I have been struggling with being a real Chinese person in China since I came back to the land of my birth at the beginning of this month.

I can no longer understand the menus: the dishes named in the traditional phrase or the modern common saying, such as 'Touch Hands, Through Black Hair', which is the title of a popular song but also seaweed cooked with pig's trotter. 'Mrs Green' is a dish of deep-fried dry, green vegetables. 'Why is it Mrs Green, not Miss?' I asked the waiter; he explained that 'Miss Green' is used for fresh vegetable dishes. (This is a typical Chinese philosophy – after marriage, women become dry and tasteless.) Meanwhile, 'Hero Can't Pass Beauty's Test' – the 1,500-year-old traditional sentence from a Tang poem – is tofu cooked with beef. By the way, if you are a man, don't say you like to eat tofu *'Ai chi dou fu'* to your Chinese friends – that means you like sex.

In the internet cafe, I dare not check my emails any more because I can't understand the questions: which would you like to use, one with a mic? A webcam? A digital printer? I see lots of people, not only youths but also grey-hairs, talking to 'nobody' on their computer, their body language dancing.

On the street, strange voices appear: an old man telling a family story; young girls singing; a military commander reprimanding a soldier, 'Wake up and go to work!'; an emperor ordering a concubine; even Chairman Mao's voice can be heard:

'People's Republic China stands up in the world.' All of these are modern Chinese ringtones!

I can see I have become hopeless in the eyes of my friends; lost in the streets that are too new to be marked on the map; lost in translation in pubs, coffee shops and restaurants; lost in the traditional Chinese health centres with their 'knowledgeable shower', 'historical massage', 'generations medical soup' and 'spiritual tea'.

'You are much more Chinese than me,' I said to my British friend Tim Clissold, the author of *Mr China*, when we met in Beijing. He laughed and told me of his experience in London. Last year, after 16 years working in China, he was thinking of moving back to England. But after just a few weeks in his homeland he changed his mind; because he couldn't drive there – his technique was too 'Chinese' for British roads and his car had been bumped too many times.

Equally, an extract from *Mr China* shows why I am not a modern Chinese:

I had just caught the tail end of the planned economy, where Beijing still tried to manipulate the minutiae of China's vast economy. At times, it might take half an hour to persuade a receptionist to let me stay in a hotel. She'd say that it was full and that there were no rooms available. At first I was puzzled and went away wondering where all the guests were, but I figured out that under the planned economy it made no difference whether a hotel was full or empty and if there were guests there would be more work to do. Since everything was owned by the state no one cared . . .

Sometimes I had to persuade a shop assistant to sell me something that I could see behind the counter; I'd go into a restaurant and they'd tell me that there was no rice, or I'd go to a bar and they'd pretend to be out of beer. I even found a restaurant in Xi'an that closed for lunch. But after a while I learned to probe and question, cajole and persuade – and never to give in! So I barged into kitchens in restaurants to find something to eat and went upstairs in hotels in search of an empty room; I grabbed whatever I needed from behind shop counters and searched sheds for bicycles to hire. Even going to buy veg-etables was a challenge but I sensed a rapport with the people I met; it was almost as if they enjoyed the game of wits and they often gave a laugh or a smile once they finally gave in.

That was China 15 years ago. Could you tell me of another country that has changed so much in such a short time?

6th May 2005

There are still students in China who believe babies come out of their mothers' tummy buttons

I read a joke in a newspaper when I was in China last week. An 11-year-old boy asks his father: 'Dad, where did I come from?' 'Your mother and I picked you up from a very special street,' the father tells him in a serious voice.

Then the boy goes to his grandfather. 'Grandpa, where did my father come from?' he asks.

'God knows your grandmother and I love children, so he sent an eagle to drop your father, your uncles and your aunt in front of our door, one by one, at different times.'

'But, why do all your children take after you, not God, and how could he remember to drop similar-looking children in front of your door when he must have been busy doing this all over the world?' The boy can't stop asking questions.

'Ah, but because he is God, he can manage it. Sorry, I have to go.' And the grandfather rushes off.

A week later, the father checks his son's homework, which is about his family history: 'It is very strange what happened in my family; I don't know why, but the previous two generations had no sex at all.'

I laughed and laughed.

Sex was forbidden in Chinese culture after the beginning of the Song dynasty in the 10th century. We had had many books on the subject but they were treated as health handbooks for the rulers, and ordinary people were never allowed to read them.

Most Chinese still believe that thinking and talking about

sex is 'dirty and bad', even between married couples. For a thousand years, family, school and society have taught us to think like this. Therefore many Chinese have grown up in total ignorance.

When I was interviewing women in China before 1997, I was told by vast numbers that they had tried to use plasters to stop the bleeding when they had their first period. Almost none of them said she was happy and excited at becoming sexually mature.

And I am not joking when I tell you that, even now, many university students believe babies come out of their mothers' tummy buttons. China started sex education in primary schools in 2002. I was curious to know who the first group of teachers would be. I was told that some were politics teachers – that is very good, I thought, at least students won't take long to learn about sexual politics once they're teenagers. Some were sports teachers – that is not bad either, I thought, I could see the link between sport and sexuality, and there's a poetic link in Chinese culture. But some teachers were made to do it as no one else would take the job.

At first, lessons were very embarrassing, with neither teachers nor students understanding the diplomatically chosen language. Then questions were taken home, but feedback from parents was furious – how dare you teach my kid such a dirty lesson! Sexual hooligans!

To be honest, this is something that is hard for a middle-aged Chinese woman to feel relaxed and natural about overnight. My heart starts pumping and I go bright red when people mention sex during my public talks. So I can't believe that our charity, Mother's Bridge of Love, has decided to hold an art exhibition called *Walnut Series – Sex in Chinese Culture*.

Everybody was shocked when we first glimpsed Chinese

artist Xu Zhong-ou's paintings. He once taught in Maryland, US, where he would gather some of his students under a walnut tree. Whereas most food in Chinese art traditionally carries a symbolic meaning (peaches represent longevity, pine nuts fertility), the walnut appealed to him as a pure (qingbai) medium. He encouraged his students to use the walnut as an unexplored source of artistic creation. This inspired him to produce his own representations of walnuts, in which he found an elusive expression of sexuality.

It was the western volunteers who first pointed out: 'Those paintings are so sexy!' At first, the young Chinese volunteers were too shocked to speak, until suddenly they became very open about sex.

I was quite worried about this un-Chinese title and asked the young Chinese volunteers if we should be leading people to see sex, even if it is infused with Chinese subtlety. They shouted: come on, old Xinran, it is time for we Chinese to tell the west: we have a very rich sexual knowledge and strong human sensuality in our culture.

I know they must be right. Please go and have a look, I would love to hear your views. You can tell me at xinran@mother bridge.org.

> *The Walnut Series – Sex in Chinese Culture*
> was exhibited at the Royal China, 13 Queensway,
> London W2 4QJ, in May 2005.

20th May 2005

The chatroom gives Chinese women a chance to be open and express their true thoughts

I have never been to an internet chatroom before – not because of any smart reasons, only because of my poor grasp of computer technology. But it was suggested that visiting one might give me some insight into the minds of young Chinese women.

'No one makes up her opinion, in the way women normally do in the office, on the street, or even at home, using carefully chosen words to conceal their true thoughts. It's like the way you don't know what some women really look like under all their heavy makeup. But in a chatroom, they say what they want to – nakedly and very honestly,' a bookstore assistant in Beijing said to me, while her right hand patted books again and again, a gesture that means 'trust me'. So I did.

The Chinese chatroom I visited, www.qq.com, was already full of 'Wang-Min'– internet obsessives – fighting over the issue of 'how to view love affairs'. I immediately regretted that I had not visited the site earlier. It is a really good place to find 'freedom of the press' from Chinese women: their words are so sharp they could cut your mind.

'Who knows you haven't had a love affair? Can you guarantee that you will never have a love affair? Don't be naive, no love is true, no human being is faithful!' – Free lady.

'Would this "Free lady" allow her husband to have another lover?' – Love defender girl.

'Why not, if we both don't want to be trapped by that piece of paper, a marriage certificate.' – Free lady.

'Then, why do you need marriage?' – Love defender girl.

'Because it meant we could give our children a family name and formal parenting, as everybody does in this society.' – Free lady.

'I see, you are a hypocrite! You think your children will be blind or that they could put up with your hideous behaviour. I don't. I think you have no right to be a parent at all!' – Love defender girl.

'What's the difference between close friends and lovers? Not much at all, you need more than one person to share your pressure and happiness, and even the physical needs in your life. Why should we only enjoy our bodies within marriage? Emotionally and physically, our needs are the same! Sex is not only for love, love does not only mean sex . . . little kid.' – Free lady.

'I would like to see if your daughter follows your example, and how you will feel when she brings several lovers to see you, or maybe she could take over your lover . . . Who knows what could happen to her – a daughter of yours – you are such an evil woman!' – Love defender girl.

I was so delighted to see these words from Chinese women talking so openly on the internet.

Many of my Chinese journalist friends are Wang-Min, too. 'Most of us just use these chatrooms to play at "freedom", which we couldn't do anywhere else. We go there to have some enjoyable arguments, to find new words, fresh language, and exercise our brains. Our freedom had been shackled for too long. Don't imagine you can have freedom all in one go, it is more like an immune system that needs to be built up over time,' one said.

The next thing was for me to try out a topic in a chatroom. I asked a very old question: 'Do you believe Chinese women could ever be equal to men?'

The fighters appeared from nowhere.

'It is impossible, until men can give birth to a baby!' – Rain bell.

'Why not, women can use their flexible brains in exchange for man's labour!' – Tree roots.

'Why do we need equality? Men are mountains, women are water, and the difference between them is good – we wouldn't have that if we were living in an equal world. Women and men should be not equal, so that we can have something we need and yearn for from each other.' – Rubbish bank.

'Let's see this equality in our basic human existence. We need each other for human reproduction, to live. What is the meaning of being a man or a woman? That is dictated by nature – men should be strong, even violent; women should be soft even to the point of tears, that is a kind of female beauty. So, don't destroy this world with your stupid equality!' – Sky eyes.

'I wonder, could women and men ever understand each other? Has this world given us any opportunity to see real equality between women and men since the time of the western God to the Chinese revolution?' – Question leaves.

The messages didn't stop flooding in until I left the Chinese chatroom. Maybe it is a debate that will rage to the time of our great-great-granddaughters.

3rd June 2005

Socks are a status symbol – does that mean barelegged westerners are all peasants?

'Why do you wear stockings in summer?' one of my students once asked me. I'd never been asked or even thought about this before. 'You know, western women only wear stockings in summer for major celebrations or meeting the Queen. But you wear them every day just for teaching – even in hot weather.' The student was a British man in his 40s, who had come to improve his Chinese writing. 'Do your women really not wear stockings in summer when they are out in public?' I asked him. 'Would they turn up to a formal meeting with bare legs?'

He rolled his eyes. I could see he meant: 'Everyone knows that.'

Afterwards, I realised what he said was true. I began to notice many western women not even wearing socks in the cold, wet London winter. Another teacher, who is Malaysian Chinese, told me she could tell who comes from less developed countries by the wearing of socks or tights in summer.

But I am Chinese. I have been told how important it is for us to wear socks to show you are from a good, educated background. That is why socks often appear in our Chinese stories. During the 1960s in the north China countryside, where it often reaches minus 20C in winter, a girl worried so much about dirtying her pair of new thick socks through her broken shoes, that she lost two toes to frostbite while walking to her wedding.

In the 1970s in south China, where it reaches more than 35C in summer, a woman going for an interview in a factory couldn't afford a pair of new thin socks and had to wear her winter socks despite the sweltering heat. In the 1980s there was a well-known sign that would hang on the doors of some of the first rich houses to be built. 'Don't worry about your holey socks, I have some too.' People were put off visiting friends who had beautifully decorated homes as it would mean taking off their shoes and exposing their threadbare socks. By the 1990s, most city girls had a drawer just for socks, but for rural girls a pair is still a big gift.

On my radio show, just before I moved to England in 1997, I received a phone call from a mother and her teenage daughter. 'Xinran, I can't tell you how much my daughter has squandered. She has two pairs of gloves for winter and buys new socks every year!'

'But I am still growing and why should I wear the faded clothes you gave me and even your cast-offs? Life has changed . . . can't you see?'

'I don't believe you should waste things.'

'What have I wasted?'

I had to stop their arguing: 'Respect for the old is one of our better customs. So we should listen to the mother first, then the daughter.'

'Please ask my daughter how many school bags she has used since she went to secondary school two years ago and how she could ruin one pair of socks after wearing them twice? Why is thrift laughed at? Why is poor treated as ugly?' The mother's voice was very sad.

'Mum, why do you never try to understand me? I did go through that pair of winter socks quickly, but they had been worn by you for more than 10 years already!' The daughter then burst into tears.

This year I was asked by some friends in Beijing: 'Why do

some foreign women not wear socks? Are they poor?' I couldn't answer their questions with my limited knowledge of the west. 'I am sure they are all educated and are not peasants. But why don't they understand public health, and allow bad smells to be let out?'

'They don't care about showing off ugly toes, do they?'

'It's terrible how our Chinese girls have started ditching their socks in public too, thinking it's fashionable.'

'What have you learned about western culture? You can't even work out why they don't wear socks in summer! Poor Xinran.' Help!

17th June 2005

There is no point worrying about feeling down. Life benefits from both happiness and suffering

Before I met Qi-Qing, the CEO of Kery Bio-Pharma in China, I had imagined her as 'the Chinese uniformed business woman'. Her company engages in bio-pharmaceutical, preventive medicine, medical nutritional products and the research and production of a skincare range using spiral algae. She is a firm believer that a business enterprise should have a strong social responsibility, which is why Kery Bio-Pharma has been working to help relieve poverty in China's remote regions.

As I sat waiting to speak to her at Kery's headquarters in Beijing, I pictured her as a typical Chinese career woman. Ten minutes later, when she had still not appeared, I started to believe I had got the right picture of her. But I knew I was wrong the minute I heard her steps. They sounded so gentle and quiet, so unlike the rushed, heavy steps of most successful Chinese businesswomen.

She greeted me in a gentle, rhythmic voice. It reminded me of what a Chinese philosopher once said: 'A few right, soft words can match a thousand hard, powerful ones.' So many other female managers only know to use strong words to get their staff to work, thinking they have to replicate the male way.

Then Qi-Qing sat down facing me, with her arms on the table. Her manicured hands opened a notebook and removed the top from her pen, like two flowers opening and waving. Every action was very ladylike.

I was so surprised by her: her beautiful face, its skin clearly carefully cared for because it did not show her age at all; the way she wore her hair made you dream of how long it could be; a cream silk scarf with flower-stars wrapped around her neck, matching her navy sweater perfectly.

This is not the image of a typical powerful Chinese woman, queen of healthcare, an economic fighter and mad worker, who never has time to think of her family and female needs, with no feel for makeup and style. Instead of wasting time talking about how to be a successful woman, we just had a chat.

Qi-Qing's only son is studying in England for his MA. Mother and son talk a lot on the phone. He is very depressed by some western textbooks which talk of China as an unknown country. Like most Chinese students who come to the west, he has not only suddenly realised how different the cultures are, but is also shocked by how little westerners know about China, going against everything Chinese students are led to expect from their history books and the Chinese media.

I could see pride in Qi's eyes when she talked about her son. She told me that she does not worry about him feeling lost and unhappy because she believes that life can benefit from both happiness and suffering. As an example, she said she had built up a strong mind and a warm heart from her unforgettable and unrepeatable childhood experiences in the Cultural Revolution.

I asked her about her 'Women's Health Garden' – a women's club that she set up just as she became successful when she needed more energy for her business development. Her eyes moved from my face to the window, and after a while they moved back to me and she said in a very sad voice: 'As you know, as Chinese women of our age, there is so much that we never speak about; we couldn't before; even now, we still use our natural female conversational skills to be a good woman in other people's eyes, to be good mothers to our children, and to be good wives to our husbands, who continue working their old traditional ways.

'I thought we must do something to help people unleash painful and angry thoughts, otherwise it could be too late. There are too many women who have paid with their lives and their health by keeping silent in the past.'

I asked her one last question. 'What is your husband's reaction to what you are doing for women?'

Her answer? 'Can we not talk about it?'

1st July 2005

English schoolchildren have shown me that China has much to learn about the joy of education

I was invited to the 2005 Children Performance in Manchester last Friday. As you know, my knowledge of this country is so little – a grain of sand in a big desert – that I didn't really understand what was happening there at all, even during the opening ceremony. I thanked people on the stage in front of an audience of hundreds, including local governors and a master of ceremonies, before they performed my play, *Sky Burial*, along with another one called London 1945.

I didn't know why they had picked *Sky Burial* for the Manchester Arts Education Initiative; I didn't know so many primary schools had produced so many different shows of *Sky Burial* since last September; I didn't know how the directors made those young British children work on such a historical story about completely foreign cultures – Chinese and Tibetan.

I was totally sucked into the performance by a group of 13 to 17-year-old students of St Peter's RC High School. I forgot that it was me who had written the story, after spending eight years doing research, during which I conducted almost 100 interviews in order to excavate and confirm the 30 years that a Chinese woman spent living in northern Tibet. At the end, I stood and bowed again and again to those teenage actors and actresses, on a stage of that size for the first time in their young lives.

The next morning, I attended a rehearsal of another *Sky Burial*, by the Advanced Performing Art Centre, made up of 30 primary and high schools. I met Peter Wilkinson, the director of all those children's plays, a man described as 'shy but mad on children's creative art work'. We didn't have time to talk because he was directing the play all morning:

'Take up the whole of the stage when you are running in the rain,' he said. The children scattered immediately, their body language saying 'escape'.

'Shu-when, you have lost Kejun – the one you love so much, what do you feel now?' A sad expression appeared on the 13-year-old actress's face.

'Now, you are on the way to Tibet where there is high air pressure, you feel very ill.' All the kids on the stage cried out with difficult breathing sounds.

'Commander, where are your shoes?'

'I forgot to wear them,' the little nine-year-old 'commander' replied.

'How could you lead your trip to Tibet without shoes?'

'I have two pairs!' one 12-year-old 'lama' raised his hand.

'What's your size?'

'Four!'

'It is too small, he needs five.'

'Mine are size five, I can give them to the commander, because I will become a sheep!'

'Thank you, sheep! Soldiers, you don't know what's happening to you when someone is killed next to you; you are so frightened – not just sitting there relaxed and chatting.'

All the soldiers started to scream out loud with fear.

'Saierbao, your daughter Ni is naughty, she won't join your family to pray, you are her mum, you have to teach her . . .' The little mum guided her daughter to the family prayer with the actions of a real mother.

'Hey, Crow, you can't take your head off all the time . . . you're alive!'

I laughed and laughed for hours at their exchanges – I never knew it could be such fun to watch children's rehearsals. Most Chinese people believe that the only way to work with teenagers is by shouting in a military-style voice. Therefore, I always saw angry teachers with poor, shaking kids preparing their beautiful stage shows in China. We thought shouting was good for our children, as part of their education. I wish I could pass this feeling on to Chinese parents and teachers: Believe that our children can give great pleasure when we know how to enjoy things with them.

'Birds, don't stop there just for pecking, you should fly, fly free everywhere to cover the sky . . .' Wilkinson was still waving his arms, his voice still lively after 10 hours' directing.

After two days, I learned that the Manchester Arts Education Initiative chose *Sky Burial* because it introduced pupils to two remote cultures. The narrative also allows for an idealistic approach to the China/Tibet conflict to be placed alongside, allowing some understanding of the problems involved without dwelling too much on the horrors.

Thank you, all members of the *Sky Burial* performance team of Manchester for building such a cultural bridge between China and Britain.

15th July 2005

Ears, lips, fingers, toes: Chinese men used to check them all in the search for the perfect wife

Possibly you know that most Chinese women had no freedom to choose their husbands before the 1940s. It was the men who did the choosing.

Sometimes, the woman was chosen from a list of surnames, enabling unions for the sake of family power or business.

Potential husbands also enjoyed a 'Chinese male right' to physically inspect those girls offered up from the lower classes. This was deemed an eminently practical and sensible way to choose a mate and breed a family. I learned about the 'right of physical inspection' from many classical Chinese novels and historical books, but I didn't know what it entailed and meant until I had a special guest for my radio show call-in, in the 1990s.

He was a medical doctor. I had invited him on to talk about 'how to get to sleep after a bad day'. After a few calls, an old lady's voice came on the line: 'Could you, Doctor, advise my son on how to choose his wife through physical inspection?'

'Hello,' I said to her. 'I can see you love your son and care about his marriage very much, but I am sure he will find the right woman to love through his own taste and beliefs. I don't think it is necessary to use the old tradition of physical inspection to find a wife.'

I tried to stop her old-fashioned talk – by law, broadcasters were expected to uphold the voice of revolution and liberation. But, in truth, I wanted to use the opportunity to learn more about physical inspection.

'Listen!' she cried. 'You have no idea how little Chinese traditional knowledge you have, all of you. You don't know how to get a better family with this kind of advice.'

'Should we cut her line off?' the programme controller asked me on another line.

'Don't worry,' I said. 'It could be good for us to learn from older generations if they don't speak against the Party. I will take responsibility for it.'

'Come on, Doctor! You know it as a part of your Chinese medical studies, don't you?' the old lady caller continued.

'Um . . . yes, I know, but . . .' he looked to me for the permission.

Yes, please, I nodded.

'OK,' he said. 'Physical inspection was a very important part of Chinese male culture before the 1940s. The ancient Chinese believed the human body was full of information about the personality of an individual and could be used for checking unmarried girls:

'Lowered eyes, unsmiling: she might hide her true thoughts.

'Raised eyes, smiling: she could be flirtatious.

'Nose like a hook: she might be after your family's money, but it could mean she is frugal.

'Curled lips: she is very negative and will nag.

'Soft ears: she is too soft-hearted and overly generous with money.

'High forehead: she comes from a very talented background.

'Curved back: she could bring shame on her family.

'Long fingers with both little fingers straight: she should have beautiful legs.

'Big hips with small waist: she will bear a boy and many more children.

'Small, thin, narrow feet: she should belong to a wealthy family background even if she is poor.

'The second toe longer than the big toe: she could have a difficult relationship with her mother-in-law.

'Smooth, pale, soft skin: she could have a rich past generation on her mother's side.'

Later, as we left the studio, I asked the doctor: 'How many physical inspections did you perform until you found your wife?'

'None, she was given to me by her father, the head of my hospital.' He rolled his eyes.

'Lucky you! What about your mother-in-law? Was she chosen by physical inspection?' I asked.

'You want to know the truth?' he asked. 'She has almost everything the opposite of good physical characteristics.'

'But why didn't your father-in-law use physical inspection for his own marriage when it was popular in his time?' I asked.

'He said his mother told him: the best choice of a wife, is that you must make sure no one else wants your wife as a lover, then you are safe and will be with her forever. That's how he tried to persuade me to marry his daughter!'

29th July 2005

The English break the ice by talking about weather, but the Chinese choose food

The weather is generally what you talk about with the British as a safe way to start a conversation or if you have nothing much else to say. But what about with Chinese people? That'll be food or health.

'Have you eaten?' '*Ni chi le ma?*' is the most important, most popular sentence in the Chinese language, used wherever and whenever, even if you just meet someone in the street at midnight. It is not necessary to answer precisely when you ate or what you had, a simple 'yes, I have' or '*chi le*' is enough. That means you are not hungry, your life isn't bad; it also means you have nothing much to talk about or you are in hurry. If you answer 'not yet' '*mei ne*' or 'what about you?' '*ni ne?*', that means you want to keep that person's attention. Or if you want to tell them something but not necessarily about food, then you could go on 'why not?' '*wei shen ma?*'

When you hear a Chinese person say, 'You look so tired, are you OK?', please don't be upset. It's not that you really look terrible. It is just our way of showing you how much we care about you. It's a way of saying we respect and admire you – you are a great person who is still working or meeting friends even though you are so tired and look terrible.

I am sure it is very difficult for westerners to accept, especially if you *are* tired and really feel terrible but don't want anyone to notice. It can all be very embarrassing.

Toby, my husband, had an accident in Argentina four years ago when he fell from a horse. He broke his left arm, shoulder bone and one rib. Before going to pick him up from the airport, I told the Chinese student who was staying with us: 'Please try to be polite and patient with this English man who must be in great pain and needs help.' But I forgot to warn him of the culture difference. The student was such a kind boy and probably thought a lot about what to say.

'Oh, my God! Toby, you look unbelievably miserable!' the boy shouted out as soon as we walked into the flat. Toby's face dropped. Before I had a chance to stop him, he continued his polite chat: 'Poor Toby, your eyes are both so bruised, like a Chinese panda!' Toby's eyes started burning. I went behind Toby and started waving my arms – stop, stop! He misunderstood and carried on: 'Yes, I can see your body is swollen like a big bear!' Then to help his basic English, he used body language – he started walking like a bear. I can't tell you how embarrassed Toby was. I felt it too, because I had learned a little bit about the difference in British and Chinese cultures.

In the following months, during Toby's recovery, I had many calls and emails – my Chinese friends really got a chance to tell us how much they cared. One western friend asked me: 'Why are your Chinese friends so "excited" by other people's health problems?'

Westerners don't understand why food and health have become such a popular topic in Chinese daily life. This comes down to more than 5,000 years of Chinese history. As far as I understand, you need to go back to historical records from about 1300 BC, when Chinese rulers started to tell people what you could or couldn't say or do. Beliefs and religion? No, you needed only believe in the ruler. Personal opinions about the society you live in? No, you were just a small cog with no need to think. Sexuality? No, that was too private to be talked about. Law? Nothing to discuss, the ruler's words were law! And so food and medicine occupied a big part of Chinese culture. Most Chinese people won't bring flowers and wine to you when they visit your home in China, but they will carry lots of tonic for your overall health.

But, I have to say, I still can't work out why the British, who have been living in a much further advanced civilisation, still choose the weather as a safe way to start their conversation.

12th August 2005

Why do old men, who need sticks to walk, open doors for healthy middle-aged women?

At the end of this month, I will have been living in London for eight years, a sixth of my life. I have experienced so much in those eight years in a foreign country amid so many foreign cultures – happiness and sadness, surprise and shock. I would need more than three books to tell the whole story.

It began at Heathrow airport. After queuing for a long time at customs, we spent more than half an hour learning how to start being 'an independent Chinese, needing no foreigner's help' just to find the right exit. 'How do we get out of this airport?' 'Way out.' What does that mean? Finally, we got in a taxi. 'Where are you going, darling?' the driver asked. Oh, my God, we had found a sexual hooligan! We looked at each other fearfully, because in China only your husband or sexual hooligans use the word 'darling'. 'Hollow,' we answered coldly. We thought we had said Harrow, short for Harrow Road. In China you don't need to add 'road', you just use the name of the road by itself. 'Hollow.'

'Hollow to you too, you beautiful ladies!' replied the cab driver. 'Where are we going? Have you got a piece of paper with the address?' He was obviously an experienced taxi driver and stopped the car to sort us out. We had only driven a few metres.

'Dress?' My friend said to me in Chinese. 'I know what this English word means, but why is he asking about our clothes? I think we have met a bad man, we should get out of this taxi.' She was so frightened, she could not wait for an answer. I held on to her with one hand and with the other passed the piece of paper with the address to the driver. When we reached the hotel, he dropped us by a tiny back door. We had done more than four loops of the street because we could not read Roman numerals but he did not charge us the extra. What we had been told in China was not true; in fact, taxi drivers in capitalist countries are better and far more professional than our socialist ones. It was the first difference we came across between what we saw and experienced here and what we had been told in China.

Shopping was not an enjoyable pastime for us – two Chinese women with a Chinese income. After a few days our shining black hair, which had been looked after weekly by a hairdresser in China, became like dry grass; our smooth Asian skin, which had looked so young, never belying our true age, became rough and old; our Chinese stomachs, which in our motherland had always been fed fresh fish, vegetables and fruits, became greedy and unhealthy. Frozen chicken, meatballs and tinned fruit became part of our everyday diet. The price we paid for our cheap London lifestyle was damaged bodies.

The first time I returned to China, my Chinese friends were very honest. 'Oh, my God, Xinran, where have you been? I thought you went to Great Britain, that developed country? Why do you look as if you've just come back from the impoverished Chinese countryside? What's happened to you?'

The difference in culture and customs really made me feel crazy and dizzy, but it touched me as well. At the beginning, I was so embarrassed by people who kindly kissed my hand or face, and hugged me. I didn't understand why these old gentlemen, who needed sticks just to walk, were opening the door for me, a healthy middle-aged woman, with neither a charming young face nor an attractive figure. I was totally lost when some western friends pointed out that I could 'invade their privacy' after I tried to help them in the best Chinese way, which is never to tell people if you want to help them – just do it. I was moved to tears when a stranger came up and asked, 'Are you OK? Do you need any help?' as I watched some children playing. I was missing my son, whom I had left behind in China that first year I came to London. Now I am surrounded by friends from different countries and different cultures.

My life has changed so much. It is true that sometimes I am still treated as an uneducated refugee, because I am Chinese. But I have published two books in more than 30 languages; I work for the media in so many different countries, I have set up a charity, MBL, for westerners who want to know about Chinese culture, be it because it is part of their roots, or simply because they are interested. I have been giving a lovely image of Britain as my second home to my family and friends, but, in the end, nothing can replace China for me as my first and proud motherland.

2nd September 2005

Even now, many Chinese find it impossible to see Mao as anything but a smiling presence

'I can make the Queen laugh or frown!' a Chinese student boasted during an Asian students' drinks party at my flat. Then she used a £10 note to show how she could change the Queen's expression from a big laugh into a frown simply by making two folds in the note.

'Have you tried this on Chinese money with Mao's face? How would his face look?' asked a western guest. 'Oh, let's try it! Mao's face must be very funny.' Some of the students became very excited.

I, too, was curious to see what Mao's face would look like. I had never seen him make any public display of anger or sadness. Even though people have painted him very differently, all have shown him smiling, unceasingly. Sometimes, I have wondered if this is because no one was allowed to take photos in Mao's moody period. Or perhaps it is because no one has had the chance to steal photos showing his angry or sad expressions from the Communist party's office in Beijing, entry to which involves getting at least three red stamps and filling in forms.

So I raised my hand to tell the students that I had a Chinese note with Mao's face on it. I was stopped by the middle-aged woman next to me. 'Don't be silly, Xinran,' she said. 'Do not let them deface Mao, it is not good for you.'

'It's just a joke,' I said. 'A game with young people. No one would think we were doing it for a political reason. And this is London, not China, and we are free to have our own views.' I went to get the note.

She stopped me before I could hand the note to the students. 'Do you want to go back to China again?' she asked.

'Of course,' I said. 'You know I go there more than twice a year.'

'Do you want to be hated by the Chinese?'

'You think the Chinese would hate me for playing a game with Mao's face? Do you believe they still regard Mao as God?' I was surprised by her attitude; she is, after all, a career woman living in the west, has been abroad since 1992 and has family with a Dutch man.

'You have been moulded by the western media, which has hardly any positive press about China and the Chinese. You often go back to China, so tell me why Mao's picture still hangs on the walls of so many people's houses, shops and offices. You think it is because the Chinese government orders them to display them, or because those people have never heard western views? Or do you think they don't know that Mao did terrible things to his people and how much he damaged his country? Be honest to our history, Xinran. I know your family has lost people under Mao's cruel policies, I know your parents were sent to prison for years and you suffered in the Cultural Revolution as an orphan.

'I am sorry to remind you of your unhappy memories. But don't look down on what Mao did for Chinese national pride, and for those poor parents in the early 1950s. I feel it is unfair to Mao.'

I stopped her. 'What about the millions of Chinese who died under his rule, because of his policies, in the 50s and 60s?'

'If westerners still believe their God is just after he flooded the world for his own purpose, or George Bush could invade Iraq with growing numbers of deaths for his campaign for moral good, why shouldn't Chinese believe in Mao, who did lots of positive things for the Chinese but also lost lives for his own mission for good?' Her voice grew angry.

'Give it to me,' said a student, snatching the note from my hand.

'I told you, don't let them use Mao's face to play with!' She was so angry that she left at once.

I was so shocked by her loyalty to Mao that I couldn't enjoy the game with Mao's face and the note.

A few weeks ago I heard some news. Peasants near Beijing, who had been campaigning since 2003 to stop a power station being built on their land, were attacked and six of them were killed by an armed gang. It was said to have been arranged by corrupt local officials.

I rang a journalist friend in Beijing to ascertain exactly what had happened. He told me what he had heard from a local news report: 'Many wounded peasants held Mao's picture and cried, "This would never have happened when Mao was alive."'

All of this made me think that it would be very difficult for a lot of Chinese people to change Mao's face in their memory or in their hearts – even in a time when their children were happy to play a game with a picture of Mao's face on a banknote that would have seen them jailed when Mao was alive.

9th September 2005

My mother's heart attack has shattered our dreams of finally getting to know each other

I am in China with my mother, who had a heart attack three weeks ago. She is sleeping in bed number 37 in the 20th department at the First Hospital of Nanjing. I am watching her as I write: her breathing is more out than in – with five tubes linking hanging bottles and machines to her tiny body – and she is covered by a sheet.

You would not believe that in her 20s this woman was one of the best dancers at Beijing military base. Her grey hair is hidden in the pillow and looks so lifeless that no one could imagine it as it was in her 30s, shining black and stylishly wrapped in bright silk. Her skinny hands are punctured by needles, making it almost impossible to believe they drew many designs of modern engineering from the 1950s through to the 90s.

I delve into my memory to dig out the old, lively images I have of her, remembering the stories others have told me about her and what I have seen in photos. I have to keep reassuring myself that she is still alive by looking at those green jumping lines and the flickering numbers on the screen, the sounds of the oxygen supply and drops of medicine.

Never in my life have I had a chance to look at my mother so close up and in such detail. Thirty days after I came out of her womb, I was sent to live with my grandparents, like so many millions of other Chinese children. Then, when I was seven and a half, I was sent to a school at my parents' military base. I lived with my parents for just two weeks before the

Cultural Revolution took place. They were both then sent to different prisons. As black-listed kids 'looked after' by red guards, my younger brother and I hardly saw them again over the next 10 years. Then I was educated and worked in cities far from where she lived.

Three years ago she rang me and said she had never given me a family birthday party and she wanted to organise one for me – her almost-50-year-old daughter.

Unfortunately, it is still a dream, like so many others we have: to make a trip together to see how China has changed since her childhood; to visit relatives in Taiwan and America, all of whom left China in the 1940s, and whom we heard about from family chat but never met; to go window shopping for toys and imagine what we would have liked to play with if she and I were both children now, because neither of us had a proper childhood (as a capitalist's delegate daughter, she was caught up in the civil war between the National party and the Communist party); to sit down together to make tablecloths for her house in Nanjing and my flat in London, as so many Chinese women do, providing handcrafted works of beauty for their lovers and family members.

But, above all of these, what we really want is the time and energy to be brave enough to open up our past to each other. As mother and daughter, we have so much we do not know about each other. So many wheres, whats and hows from when we were separated for all those years by the Cultural Revolution. We have been scared to tell the truth.

It is much harder for my mother. I know one of her secrets: in a cupboard in her bedroom, she has many new dresses given to her in the 1970s – she refuses to wear them, so that she can forget her past when the beauty and bright was replaced by dark and suffering.

I do not know whether or not we could talk about our deep, hidden past at the end of her life because I am told by her doctor that she is too weak to have any emotional conversation.

Every morning, I wake her up quietly so that her temperature and blood pressure can be taken. She has very little breakfast, but I still go and get two or three newspapers and three bunches of lilies for her new day and a fresh smile. After her daily treatment we have a 10-minute walk while we talk about the news. I am so touched by her trust as she allows me to wash her hair and clean her body. She never complains, even though the first doctor made a big mistake and delayed her heart operation. Sometimes she even looks funny – like a child trying to steal a tiny bit of 'forbidden meat' from my plate for her 'greedy happiness'.

Oh, my dear mum, please go on with your beliefs and your life for both you and me. I who dream of being your daughter wrapped in your arms.

I always feel that I never thank my family and friends enough. I would like to take this chance to thank the following people from my heart:

Toby – my husband, who knows what the Chinese DO eat and has shared so much Chinese culture with me.
PanPan – my son, who has started choosing his Chinese meals with the background of only five years of western education.

Clare Margetson – my editor at the *Guardian*, who lit my way to this book.
Lucy Clouting – my manager at the *Guardian*, who handled my work smoothly.
All *Guardian*ers – for allowing my words into your admirable paper.

Rachel Cugnoni – my Vintage boss, who has encouraged my writing so much and also encouraged me to have my old face on the front of this book cover.
Elizabeth Foley – my editor at Vintage, who helps me not only in writing but also with my charity MBL with her heart.
Audrey Fitt, Sue Amaradivakara and all the Random House staff, who have supported me a great deal since I became their author.

All of the volunteers of MBL (The Mothers' Bridge of Love) in China, the UK and other countries, who have taught me and support my love for Chinese children with their hearts; I wouldn't have been able to write these columns without their knowledge and information.

Since the publication of her books Xinran has received a huge number of letters from the adoptive mothers of Chinese children and Chinese mothers living abroad. In response to these letters she decided to create her own charity, The Mothers' Bridge of Love, to help these women, their children, and the many children living in destitute conditions in China.

More than 55,000 western families have adopted Chinese orphans, mainly girls, since 1993. As they grow up, these children ask:
'Why didn't my Chinese mummy want me?'

Over 50% of the Chinese people live in poverty. Millions of children all around the country can only dream of a decent education. These children ask:
'How can I ever go to school?'

Meanwhile millions of overseas Chinese children hardly understand their roots. These children ask:
'What is Chinese culture?'

Xinran's charity, The Mothers' Bridge of Love, helps to find answers to these questions by building a bridge between China and the world; between rich and poor; between children's birth culture and their adoptive culture.

Please do visit the charity's website
www.motherbridge.org

MBL – The Mothers' Bridge of Love
Charity Registration No. 1105543

If you would like to send a cheque
please use the following address:

MBL
9 Orme Court
London W2 4RL
UK

If you would like to make a bank transfer or for online
payment, please send funds to:

The Mothers' Bridge of Love (MBL)
Sort Code: 400607
Account Number: 11453130
HSBC Bank
Russell Square Branch
1 Woburn Place, Russell Square
London WC1H 0LQ
SWIFT Code: MIDL GB2142E